NEPAL
AN EXOTIC TOURIST DESTINATION

Yajna Raj Satyal

ADROIT PUBLISHERS
DELHI-110 053 (INDIA)

ADROIT PUBLISHERS
C-8/2, Yamuna Vihar,
Delhi - 110 053

Nepal: An Exotic Tourist Destination

First Edition, 2001
ISBN 81-87392-12-6

Printed at Neeraj Print Services, Delhi

PRINTED IN INDIA

Published by Adroit Publishers, Delhi.

Contents

Foreword

The development of tourism in Nepal mirrors the constant growth. High rates of growth are in evidence during recent years. Nepal has now placed high priority on the development in tourism through which development in other sectors of the economy is to be achieved.

International tourism has had considerable impact on Nepal which is not uncommon in view of the smallness of the country and the rapid growth of the tourism industry. There is a greater awareness and appreciation of things Nepali, not only Cultural heritage such as temples, stupas, historical monuments but also natural heritage, arts and crafts and even locally produced beer. These, in turn, have also been affected by tourist tastes and expectations. The Nepali concept of the quality of life has also touched the influence of tourism. This is reflected not only in architectural styles of hotel building but also in the increased popularity among the Nepali urban dwellers of such leisure activities as visits to restaurants and clubs.

The tourism sector initially flourished in the Country's marginal areas, (Kathmandu Valley, Pokhara, Everest Region and some of the other tourist spots), which are primarily rich in cultural and natural attractions. The construction of tourist infrastructures such as hotels in these areas further accentuated the big concentration of facilities, employment and business. The expansion of employment opportunities is related to fulfill the demand of the hotel industry, travel and trekking agencies as a whole for a range of supporting and ancillary services. Although the number of such establishments has grown tremendously, many of them face difficulty to survive simply due to the lack of proper international marketing approach. His Majesty's Government of Nepal's policy for granting licences for such organisations and service industry is liberal and many hotels, travel and trekking, rafting, jungle safari agencies are opened to cater the tourists. The demand of job in Tourism and lack of trained power to man and manage the industry and the service sector encourages both intra- and inter-regional migration. The extent to which local people will benefit more or less than other from this employment generation depends on many factors. High level jobs go to expatriates due to non-availability of trained local staffs. To strike while the iron is hot, tourism research is of urgent need. Research means, as all we know, a careful search or investigation or systematic investigation towards increasing the sum of knowledge. Now tourism research is needed and to be carried out for pin-pointing, how far the industry is alive to its own perspective and is especially cautious of its economic benefits and its negative effects and over all significance to the country? The situation in our country, as it seems extraordinary in that the demands, constraints, risks and potentials of a fragile agricultural environment, a large urban nucleus, specially in Kathmandu Valley, an emerging housing boom and tourism are surging head on. The service industry, so far, proves to be oriented to servicing foreigners and so more induces to foreign imports, not realizing the import substitution. With all these effects on the growth of tourism in our country, no exploration and study are being made to find the specific realizations such as tourist types, the various stages of tourism development, the impact of tourism in socio-cultural affairs and effects on arts and crafts are not taken into account.

No comprehensive development in the tourism sector can be achieved and carried out unless an adequate provision is made for the supporting communities, highways, airports and other transport systems, facilities for recreation, cultural and historical preservation as well as substantial agricultural and industrial activities that support the tourism plant. In the absence of long term planning in tourism, there is no co-ordination in areas of transportation and infrastructure which has posed problems in safeguarding the social and economic soundness of the country. While embarking on any tourism planning, it is necessary to visualize issues of material benefits from tourism development, the question of economic benefits and social welfare. The most obvious and immediate benefit of tourism is the creation of jobs and the opportunity for people to increase their income and standard of living.

A small country like ours with relatively underdeveloped production facilities and infrastructure and low levels of skills among people made it difficult to carry out tourism strategies which often require well-trained cadres. It is hightime now to initiate and implement measures to consolidating the diversifying needs of foreign visitors by consolidating existing and creating new areas with proper facilities to cater for increasing number of tourists. To make the most out of tourism, the country has to follow more vigorous, active and widespread planning and suitable policy to ensure that gains from tourism development go to the most needy among the local people and not be concentrated among the few. The policy toward tourism and the degree of "control", "regulation" or "intervention" will be determined by a country's overall approach to economic and social issues and the role in tackling them.

Over the years, emphasis has been given to lure international tourists instead of simply increasing the quantity not caring for quality so as to increase foreign exchange earnings. Similarly, efforts have been made to concentrate expansion of tourism in areas where infrastructure is adequate, to create new employment opportunity and to increase the production of goods required in tourism sector, but now if possible, new tourist areas opened in different regions of the country and all materials required for the consumption by tourism sector within the country itself, in order to reduce import and strengthen indigeous industries. Regular exercises designed to emphasize the contribution, relevance and significance of tourism will also help all those in the trade to develop tourism as an industry and national benefits will be mobilized in such a way that they are distributed fairly among the population. The success of tourism plans that contribute to national goals and the extent to which the country is able to control tourism for its own benefit.

The analytical framework for the prevailing issues of the development of tourism in our country is provided attempting to take account of socio-cultural impacts for more systematic approaches. An attempt is made to represent the facts in a plain manner. Necessary facts and informations have been provided to make the subject more interesting and attractive. Constructive suggestions for any imperfection or mistakes of commission and omission will be highly appreciated and greatly entertained for making this book more comprehensive and readable in the future.

Author

1

Land and the People

Nepal's physical location and character is regarded as unique and spectacular. Barely, rectangular in shape, Nepal covers an area of 147,181 square kms, length from east to west 885 kms, breadth from south to north 144—241 kms. It is situated in the southern slopes of the mid-Himalayas, the formidable range of eternal snows. The nearest sea coast is about 1,127 km from its border. Nepal lies between north latitude, hence on the same parables as North Africa or Mexico.

Nepal is a land-locked country between India and People's Republic of China. The major part of the country is of high mountains and rolling hills. It accounts for about 83% of the total land area and the remaining 17 per cent is occupied by the flat lands of the Terai. Altitude varies from 152 m above the sea level in the Terai in the south to more than 8839 m in the northern Himalayas.

Though only 145 km in width Nepal displays a unique variety of geographical regions ranging from the tropical lowlands to the Arctic plateau. Between these gaps lay the Middle Hills, inhabited thousands of years ago, it is this traditional region of Nepali culture and history, at whose heart lies the exotic Valley of Kathmandu, embracing an exceptional culture and scenic wealth.

The Great Himalayas lies across northern Nepal topped by 8848 m. Mount Everest together with some eight snow peaks of over 8579 m and about two hundred 4877 m peaks. On the frinze of the range dwell the highland people among these the famed Sherpas who have climbed earth's highest snow peaks.

On the basis of altitude alone, the country can be divided into three natural regions:

1. *Himalaya Region*: This lies at an altitude of 4877 m to 8839 m above sea level with the snow line running at 4877 m. The Himalayan ranges like the Kumbhakarna, the Jugal and the Annapurna fan out from the east to the west. In this region, the world's famous peaks of Mount Everest (8848 m), Kanchanjangha (8586 m), Makalu (8463 m), Dhaulagiri (8167 m) and Annapurna (8091 m) are located. The Nepal Himalayas have 240 peaks, exceeding 6094 m in elevation. Eight of the world's highest giants as Mount Everest, Kanchanjunga, Lholse, Makalu Cho Oyu, Dhaulagiri, Manaslu and Annapurna lie in the Nepal Himalayas.

2. *Mountain Region*: This region is formed by the Mahabharat range that soars upto 4877 m. The Mahabharat range stretches from the Mahakali to beyond the Kosi Valley. This range of mountain rises 4877 m and its ridges hold a horizontal leaning towards the south and a gentle slope toward the north. The northern and northeastern sectors of this range are covered with dense forest. The hill regions are densely populated. The Valleys and deltas are fertile and so thickly settled. The Kathmandu Valley lies to the north of the range.

The Churia Hills, a continuation of the Siwalik range of India are covered with timber and savanna grass. This Churia Hill region begins from 1,200 meters above the sea level and covers the 15 per cent area of the country. The valley of this hills are known as "Duns" which are model of the foothill of Nepal. Southward stands the influential and ample steep bending slope known as the Bhabar. South of the Bhabar and Churia Hills is the Terai, the low fertile alluvial place.

3. *Terai Region*: The lowland at the foot of the hill covers open flat countryside and forest clad mountains. It is situated at an altitude of maximum 305 m occupies about 17 per cent of the total area of the country. It is a fertile plain stretching from east to west in the southern part of the country. The length of the Terai is about 880 kms. This region is densely populated and is highly important for its food crops.

The topography of the country is a succession of bands running along the east-west axis. To the south as mentioned above is the Terai, a flat tropical belt, an extension of the Ganges plain never more than 40 km wide. From the Terai, the land rises steeply to the Mahabharat Lekh mountain range with peaks of upto 3050 m. This is followed by the wide bank of the Central Hills, an indulating mountain area and which builds to the snow covered Great Himalayan Range whose summits from the northern boundary of Nepal in the east. Towards the west, Nepal extends beyond the Himalayan Range to the Trans-Himalayan Zone which is part of the barren Tibetan Plateau. This dramatic complex and varied topography forms the basis of the tourism attraction of Nepal. Though only 150 miles across, it has a wide variety of geographical regions, ranging from the tropical southern lowlands to the arctic Tibetan Plateau—"the roof of the world". Between these areas are the Middle Hills at whose breast lies the Valley of Kathmandu. Nepal offers within her short compass such a massive variety of attractions from the rolling plains of the Terai, skirting the foothills up the serried ranks of the mountains enclosing lush valleys through to the rising majestic heights of the Great Himalayas.

Nepal is a country of mountains and has a very pleasant climate. From the plains of the Terai to the summits of the Himalayan every type of climate is founded here. Due to extreme variation in altitudes, the country has from tropical to alpine climates. Tropical, temperate and alpine types of climate are respectively encountered in its Terai belt, midland hills and the alpine region. The Kathmandu Valley has an equable climate. But it is much colder at higher elevations. The summer is wetter than in winter in Nepal. The Monsoon season begins from June and last till September. The climate is warm and humid in summer, moist and temperate in monsoon and cold and rain-free in winter. For example, when it is summer in the hot plains of the Terai, it is the spring in the hilly regions and winter in the snow-covered Himalayas. That is why it is said that a visitor can find a climate suitable and congenial to him in the country all the year round. The varied climate creates a complex seasonality problem, but at the same time opportunities for tourism.

Nepal has composite population stemming from various racial strands. Nepal has been a melting pot of diverse linguistic and ethnic groups. The temperate highlands are the natural home of the Mongoloid tribes while the lower tropical and sub-tropical zones are the habitats of the Aryan races. Besides, these are also interesting minority ethnic groups like the Kusundas, Chepangs, Hayus and Rautes who still live in huts in the forests.

The inhabitants of higher altitudes Sherpas, Tamang, Kiratis, Limbus and Botiyas are drawn from Mongoloid stock. The Mid-lands are populated by Tamangs, Magars, Gurungs, Sunuwars, Newars, Brahamins, and Chhetries. In the inner Terai region, Tharu, Chepang, Magar and people of Aryan stock hold a dominant position.

The Nepali people and their way of life act as a major attraction to visitors and represent an important facet to cultural tourism. The Nepali warmth and friendliness towards visitors form part of their high degree of tolerance towards alien cultures and religion developed through a long history of close contact with the peoples of its neighbouring countries. Foreigners also come to see the famous characters associated with Nepal—the Sherpas, the tiger of the snow-mountain guide, the Gorkha soldiers—the gallant fighters in the world. Near about 93 per cent of the working population is engaged in agriculture and allied activities while 3 per cent is engaged in manufacturing industries.

Nepali people are warm-hearted and hospitable. International visitors are always welcomed everywhere by sweetness and gentility. As a part of their tradition of culture, the people have evolved a lofty and profound cultural and religious ideals and have developed hospitality as a natural tradition. This prodigy of traditional life style of the people has astonishing lease of cultural tourism and unique national characteristics which often appreciated by all. The elements have sprit of reverence to strangers and assisted in welcoming visitors as a national tradition. The hospitable disposition of the people has successfully evolved its own singular socio-cultural pattern. Friendliness, hospitality and sense of help are noticed everywhere. They regard foreign visitors as their honoured guests and they are pleased to make acquaintance and embrance with welcome and love. They greet all visitors with open arm and Namaste which covers the meaning of welcome and to meet them again soon.

Nepal is the only Hindu Kingdom in the world. Religion is an integral part of Nepali life. Three main religious creeds namely Hinduism, Buddhism and Tantricism prevail in Nepal. The Nepali people observe various forms of Hinduism such as Shaiva, Baishnava, Sakta, Nath and Buddhism in both tantric and non-tantric forms. Hinduism and Buddhism are both equally honoured in Nepal and the blending of the two religions into one entity have inspired and created the distinct culture of its own. Buddhism beliefs and practices date back to Nepal since the time of its founder, Gautam the Buddha who was born at Lumbini in West Nepal Terai in about 543 B.C. There are many castes and creeds in Nepal but no rigidity. There is religious tolerance everywhere. Everything is based on compromise and understanding.

The Nepali people observe many festivals and fairs than there are days in the year and these events are commonly celebrated by all peoples. The reflection of uniqueness of Nepali culture can be seen in the every day life of the people and in the works of arts and architectures. Nepal is the cultural museum where art treasures and monuments of historical interest are preserved. The arts and crafts of Nepal, inspired by Hindu and Buddhist religion are of an astonishing richness all over the country.

Kathmandu with Patan and Bhadgaon second and third cities in importance in the Kathmandu Valley constitute a rare ensemble of an architectures of great originality and quality. Innumerable temples both Stupas and pagodas and many other interesting monuments and private houses with carved doors and windows contain valuable archaelogical, historical, religious and art collection of Nepali culture. Some of these places such as Hanuman Dhoka—the old palace in Kathmandu, Durbar Square in Patan and Bhadgaon, the Pashupatinath temple, the Buddhist Stupas of Bodhnath and Swayambhunath are well known and many other places of interest like Sankhu, Chagunarain, Parping, Kertipur deserve attention. There are many national cultural centres outside Kathmandu Valley—Janakpur—birthplace of Sita, epic heroine of Ramayana and Lumbini—world known birth place of Gautam Buddha. Lumbini situated on the alluvial western Terai, is a world famous pilgrimage site in Nepal. There is historic temple of Janaki (Lord Rama's consort of Great Hindu Epic Ramayana) in the town of Janakpur in the east Terai. There are other Buddhist and Hindu shrines of Nepal in the west and eastern sides of the country which are famous for pilgrimage. Muktinath famous for Jwala Mai (Goddess of Flame) is located on a high mountain range of about 3,749 meters. Thyangloche is situated at the fort of Sagarmatha (Mt. Everest). It is about 250 kilometers north east of Kathmandu Valley. Barahachheta is the holy place of Hindu pilgrimage a few Kilometers from the main city of Biratnagar. It lies at the confluence of two rivers—Saptakosi and Kokaha. There is a temple of Lord Baraha, boar incarnation of Lord Vishnu. There is another place known as Gosainkund is renowned for its religious pond at 4360 meters above sea level to the north-west of Helambv and is 132 kilometers north-east of Kathmandu. Similarly, Manakamana is one of another most famous religious spots is located in the district of Gorkha.

Side by side with religious pilgrimage sites, the country has many scenic sports as Gorkha which is the ancestral home of Shah Kings of Nepal and is a beautiful place full of historical and scenic beauty. Pokhara Valley is another picturesque Valley which is 200 kilometers west of Kathmandu. It has lovely lakes and offers a dramatic view of Himalayan peaks. Likewise, Helambu is nearly 72 kilometers north-east of Kathmandu and is noted for the scenic beauty and salubrius climate. There is another lovely Himalayan Town of Tansen at 1371 m. above sea level in western Nepal. Then Charikot, the headquarters of Dolakha District is 133 kilometers from Kathmandu and is known for its scenic grandeur. Rapti-Valley, Chitwan is situated 120 kilometers south-west of Kathmandu. This is full of largest forest areas known for viewing rare wildlife and jungle safaris. There is Namche Bazaar which is about 241 km. from Kathmandu and famous for Sherpa Villages and Thyangboche monastery.

Here in Nepal, vacation variety is unlimited. Nepal is a Nature playground all the year round. It is a land of varied attractions for adventures and exotic pleasures as well as experiencing some of the greatest sites of South Asia's cultural sights. Trekking offers everything all within a short compass—snow-covered Himalayas and ancient Pagodas, medieval cities and typical villages. Trekking in the Himalayan slopes up to an altitude of 5,500 m is within the scope of the visitor and has developed as a major activity. There is also an opportunity to experience wildlife adventure or relax in the jungle silence of Nepal's 11 National Parks, Wildlife Reserves and Conservation Areas located in different geographic regions. Nepal also provides an endless challenge to mountaineering expeditionary teams. The number of mountaineers is increasing annually and popular peaks are looked years ahead for mountaineering. Eight of the world's eighteen peaks exceeding 8,000 m., such as Sagarmatha (Mount Everest) the highest peak in the world (8848 m), Kanchanjungha (8,586 m), Lholse (5,616 m), Makalu (8,475 m), Daulagiri (8,167 m.), Cho oyu (8,210 m), Manaslu (8,163 m), and Annapurna (8,091 m) are in Nepal. Rafting has become another major type of adventure tourism in Nepal. Rafting trips are of varying duration and usually take place on such rivers as the Trisuli, Narayani, Marshandi, Seti and Sunkosi. Many licenced agencies now organise "Combination Trips" consisting of Trekking and rafting or alternatively a rafting trip to jungle safari for wild life viewing.

Nepal dreams travel supervised holiday with excitement and novelty but relaxed enough to enable to visitor the magnificent scenery, rare wildlife, culture and religion of this fascinating part of Asia. Here too, visitor can see and enjoy such wonders as deepest gorges, snowy peaks, glacier moraines, waterfalls, hot springs, rocky as well as green mountains and a host of other famous places and sights. Best yet vacation begins the minute, the international visitor looks for travel in Nepal. Nepal vacation offers marvellous paradise. Here is where every day and every kilometer unfolds new delights and thrills. Here is where mountain terrain combines with a natural wonderland, a panorama of changing scenery, the rugged mountains, the timbered slopes of the wide sweeps of river beds, glacier carrying streams, lush green serene environs everywhere with sprouting vegetations and variety of flowers in profusion of blooms. Along with natural attractions, Nepal is famous for tradition, art and sophistication with famed old palace complex, temples and stupas, Pagodas—fascinating combination of many art and architectural styles. So, Nepal is still the only country with a continent to itself, but little else remains the same.

2

Art and Architectures

Nepal is endowed with the historical and cultural aspects of interest. Among the rich wealth of varied attractions are the historical buildings, temples and stupas which are scattered in all parts of the country. The temples and stupas are rich repositories of wood carving, metal working, terracotta and stone sculpture. The old glory and uniqueness to the cultural scene of the country and record of a long annals of native genius. The exquisite architecture and artistic decorators of Nepali temples and historical buildings that enshrine the bronze and stone images of great beauty and more often than not, great antiquity, are a unique feature of Nepal. So a journey to Nepal gives one the impression stepping back through history by many hundred years. So Nepal is the cultural storehouse where art treasures and religious monuments along with testimonials of historical interest are preserved as constant sources of attraction to international visitors. The arts and crafts of Nepal inspired by ancient Hindu and Buddhist culture are of an astonishing richness especially in the valley of Kathmandu. While speaking about a cultural efforescence of Nepal, the great and renowned scholar Mr. Christoph von Furer-Haimendorf has expressed his feeling in such as way "Though barley two hundred and fifty square miles in area this valley was at various times the scene of a cultural efforescence remarkable even in the perspective of the civilization of Nepal's neighbours, India and Tibet. Its cities, adorned with temples and palaces ranking the finest architecture of Asia, served as a meeting ground of people from both these countries, and this role of link between two different worlds engendered an unusual capacity for weaving heterogenous ethnic and cultural elements into a complex fabric of distinctive character."

Happily preserved from great migrations and invasion, Kathmandu with Patan and Bhadgaon, second and third towns in importance constitutes a rare ensemble of an architecture of great originality and quality. A large number of temples (stupas and pagodas) and thousands of other interesting monuments and private houses (carved wooden windows) are within easy reach in the oval valley of less than 250 sq. miles. Some of these places, Hanuman Dhoka—the old palace in Kathmandu, Durbar squares in Patan and Bhadgaon, the Buddhist stupas of Bodhanath and Swayambhunath, the famous temples of Pasupatinath, Taleju Bhawani, Changu Narain etc., are now well-known and visited by the tourists and many other places of interests like Sankhu, Changunarain, Parping Gokarna deserve attention.

Many buildings testify Pagoda style of architecture and numerous predominant temples and shrines of the early Lichhavian and Malla periods stand in cities and are scattered throughout the countryside and are even found in villages. Many cities and towns still carry the typical features on their Mandap (ground plan) seen not only in their urban conception, but also in the number of beautiful preserved Malla palaces and buildings. Urban towns and villages of more or less historically important still have such a wealth of original Pagoda style that the visitor feels as if he has stepped into the middle ages. The historical and artistic standard of Lichhavi and Malla period not only document the excellent standard of architectural art in this part of Asia at that time (7th century A.D.—12th century A.D.) but is a priceless cultural contribution to the history of mankind. Similar testimony is given by monasteries, gateways, pavilions and other edifices built also for enhancement of art. Most of the cities and towns consist of entire complexes covering scores of surroundings of few miles.

The most unique example of the Nepali architecture is embodied in what has been easily known as the Pagoda style of architecture. This architectural style was popular in Nepal in the middle of the seventh century. The Chinese account of Nepal (643-651) recorded in the history of the Thang Dynasty highly speaks of Nepali arts and architectures. Many scholars including Landon mentioned that Pagoda style of architecture was a Nepali invention and this style was not known in China. So far as the person like Sylvan Levi, and scholar in oriental arts and culture, has precisely pointed out that "They (Nepalese architects) have changed the arts of India, built temples and palaces which have sensed as models to the Tibetans and the Chinese, the classical pagoda hails from Nepal".

The best examples of the Pagoda style in the Kathmandu Valley are Machhendranath, Pasupatinath, Taleju, nine-stoned Basantpur Palace, Kasthamandop in Kathmandu, Hiranya Varna Mahavihar, Kumbheswar and Machhendranath in Patan and Changu Narayan, Nyatapol, Bhairavnath temple, Dattatreya Temple etc. in Bhadgaon.

Pagoda style refers to multiroofed structures with wide eaves supported by carved wooden struts, window either latticed or grilled are usually projecting while the roof is generally topped off triangular spires enclosing an unvented bell of stucco or barnished gold. The pagoda style shows the finest specimens of the architectural genius of Nepal. The most outstanding example of Pagoda style is Changu Narayan. This is one of the Valley's oldest and most famous temple constructed during the Lichhavi era, perhaps around the eighth century A.D. These Pagoda temples such as Machhendranath, a pagoda of two tired bronze roof, Basantpur Durbar or Navtalle Durbar built by King Prithvi Narayan

Shah, the great, Kasthamandap, a pagoda constructed out of a trunk of a single tree. Pashupati Nath temple of Lord Shiva, a pagoda temple with gilt roof and richly carved silver doors in Kathmandu are remarkable in their architectural supremacy. Likewise, the pagodas such as Kumbheswar temple five-tiered oldest example, first of this kind in Nepal. Hiranya Varna Mahavihar—three stoned golden temple of Lokeshwar built in the 12th century A.D. Machhendranath, the pagoda full of numerous folds of artistic skills around it, deserve attention in Patan. Bhadgaon is the home of medieval arts and architectures. Nyatapola built in 1708 A.D. is the tallest typical five storied pagoda style temple in the Kathmandu Valley, it is famous for its massive structure and finest workmanship. This is tallest in all Nepal. Thus, Pagoda style, in fact, set of a lofty standard of space and height and treatment of material, its delicacy and decoration show a stricking contrast to the massiveness and simplicity.

After Pagoda style, the Shikhara style forms yet another architectural style found in Nepal. The super-structure of the style is a tall pyramidal tower whose surface is broken up vertically into five or nine sections. The final section consists of a bell-shapped part of the top. The Krishna Mandir of Patan Durbar square is the finest example of this style. It has remarkable bas-reliefs in stone depicting war scenes from the ancient Hindu epics Ramayana and Mahabharat. It was built in the sixteenth century. This temple is enriched with Nepali craftsmanship and skill. Mahaboudha is also in more or less of this style on Terracotta moulded bricks and is known as temple of million Buddha images built in fourteenth century. This is also Nepali architectural masterpiece.

The Stupa style of architecture is another triumph of Nepal which is purely Buddhist in concept and execution. It is a hemispherical mound topped by a square base supporting a series of thirteen circular rings narrowing towards the top. These are crowned by a parasol. The four sides of the square base painted with pairs of "all seeing eyes" of Buddha. The stupa is often white-washed with lime stone. The Swayambhu and Bouddha Nath Stupas are Nepal's superb examples of the Stupa style. The Swayambhu is said to be two thousand years old, making it one of the world's oldest and most glorious Buddhist stupas. Bauddhanath is a colossal stupa, one of the biggest in the world. This stupa is inset on four sides with the all seeing eyes of Lord Buddha. Built on a huge octagonal base, the stupa is also inset with prayer wheels.

The three architectural styles are prominent (Pagoda, Shikhara and Stupa) throughout Nepal and especially in the Kathmandu Valley as the priceless testimonials of Nepali culture focussing the ideals of the two religions of Hinduism and Buddhism. Actually, the great architect of the two religions meet and mingle in Nepal and cause to develop wealth of important Hindu and Buddhist shrines ranking among the finest architectures of Asia. Tri-cities of Kathmandu Valley are for culture, tradition and art. The famed Durbar squares of Kathmandu, Patan and Bhadgaon, numerous temples and stupas display half a century in building, is a fascinating combination of many architectural styles with craftmanship in wood, metal and stone. Nepal by these singular beauty of arts and architectures is regarded as one of few countries in the world where seven world Heritage Sites are situated within 20 kilometers of radius. Kathmandu Durbar Square or most popularly known by the name of Hanuman Dhoka of Kathmandu, full of temples, palace buildings and courtyards constructed during Malla Period (12th to 18th century) which is now included in the world Heritage Sites. Similarly, Buddhist Stupa of Swayambhunath with many miniature Stupas, shrines, sacred pillars etc., the famous double-roofed Pagoda temple of gold-gilt brass dedicated to God Pashupati Nath, Buddhanath stupa, the largest Buddhist Chaitya in the world, Bhaktapur city or the city of Devotees, the home of medieval arts and architectures represented by the Durbar Square with numbers of shimmering pagodas with exquisite figures and religious symbols, Changu Narayan Temple, the rare artistic heritage from the Lichhavi period, and Patan Durbar Square, fabulous cluster of pagoda temples with carved facades and stone monoliths having bronze statues are all listed as World Heritage Sites by UNESCO.

Naturally, relics of the classic period and of the following architectural trends of 16th century are also present among the architectural pieces found in Nepal. It is better to point out that in Nepal all these architectural treasures are accompanied by combines and series of artistic works—paintings, sculptures from each respective period and are supplemented by objects of daily uses. Bhaktapur Art Gallery Collections acquaint visitors with the wide range of masterpieces of paintings. There are also original collections of period including both civil, religious and theatrical costumes which can be seen in festival and other special occassions. All these historical relics represent an immense wealth of national tradition and are valuable tourist attractions. Active handicraft, bronze and brass in Patan, pottery in Thimi, wood-carving and painting testifies that the traditional taste is still living.

The earliest examples of Nepali paintings are in the form of manuscripts illustrations on palm leaves. All serving illustrated manuscripts whether Buddhist or Hindu are illustrated with images of Gods and Goddesses around 11th century A.D. These arts presentation exercised a lasting influence on Tibetan art. Religious paintings worshipped as icons are known as Paubha in Newari and Thangkha in Tibetan. The origin of Thanka paintings may be attributed to the Nepali artists responsible for creating a number of special metal works and wall-paintings as well as illustrated manuscripts in Tibet. Besides painting, another art forms worth mentioning are wood-carving. These are numerous intricate and beautiful windows, doors, temple roof-struts and other artifacts carved entirely by hand. These forms of arts date back to fourteenth century and the beginning of Malla period. The best examples are the old Royal palaces of Kathmandu, Patan and Bhadgaon and a number of different monasteries in all over the country. The Golden Gate of Bhaktapur Durbar is a unique example of Nepali art. The over-all design is drawn with a clear conception of workmanship.

The sculptural art of Nepal not only played a prominent part in itself but also exerted influence upon the art of neighbouring countries. Huan Chwang who passed through Nepal in 637 A.D. and took down account about Nepal which was full of praise of the Nepali arts. In the same way, Chinese account of Nepal, 643-651 A.D. (History of the Thang Dynasty) highly speaks about the Nepali and their sculptural arts. A large number of ancient sculptural arts have survived up till now. The most important are the statues of the Kirat Kings and some terra-cotta figures excavated in the Terai at Tilourakot near the nativity of Gautam Buddha, other masterpieces of the 7th century presence in Archaeological Gardens, Patan and National Gallery, Bhadgaon. These are some remarkable sculptures from Lichhavi Period (5th-8th century) at Changu Narayan. This sculptural arts of 6th-10th century are also famous. Early Malla Period (11th-14th century) confine a most beautiful art treasures. Late Malla Period is regarded as the last phase of Nepali creations that the Tantric way of depiction given by images of Violent appearance. The sexual symbolism "Parts of Opposition of Tantric Buddhism" is depicted by the love making of male with female images sculpture of this period look simple and plain but decorated in grace and appearance.

There are many national cultural and religious centres outside Kathmandu Valley. The most famous are Janakpur—birth-place of Sita and Lumbini—world famous birth place of Gautam Buddha. Janakpur is an epic famed town and birth-place of Sita—wife of Rama, the hero of the epic

Ramayana. The place is renowned for its marble temple of Janaki. This famous religious place is situated 370 kilometers south-east of Kathmandu in the eastern Terai. The Rama and Sita temples are the centres of pilgrimage. The marble temple of Sita is full of artistic designs, popularly built at the cost of Rs. 900,000. Great religious festivals, pilgrimage, trade fairs and other festivities are occurred on Vivaha Panchami and Ram Navami days which fall in late March and April and Panchami in the month of December. This place is regarded as the most venerated place of worship because of Goddess Sita and Lord Rama were married in this place. So this place continues to be a great place for pilgrims from different parts of Nepal and India. This place was the capital of ancient Mithila (Videha State) in the legendary times. Mithila was ruled by Janak who was the father of Sita and also a king of great wisdom and justice. Janakpur derived its name from the wise and benevolent King Janak.

Lumbini is the birthplace of Lord Buddha, the prince of peace, compassion and non-violence. It is located in Kapilvastu District of Lumbini zone-western Terai of Nepal; 250 kilometers south-west of Kathmandu. Here the broken Ashokan pillar, remnants of an old monastery, images of Buddha's mother Maya Devi etc. are preserved which give an idea of religious and traditional skill of Nepali genius. It is the sacred place for the Buddhists and the sacred Buddhist pilgrimage site. These two places mentioned above Janakpur and Lumbini are very famous since time immemorial. We have a historical evidence that the Chinese and Japanese Buddhists travelled long distances to visit Lumbini, the birth-place of Buddha and Indians to Janakpur, braving many hardships and endurances.

There are many Gompas (Buddhist monasteries in Helambu, Thyanboche and many other places) which deserve visit to know the singular arts and architectures presented by these monasteries. These monasteries contain images and tapesteries from bygone ages, as well as a number of artifacts received at archaeological excavation sites, art galleries, museums, archives, libraries, memorials and 'monuments' of repute. The affluence of its arts and beautiful architectures in the midst of scintillating natural splendour has lent magnificance and a mystical charm to Nepal.

Unforgettable scenes and historical places with traditional artistry haven given it a distinct cultural identity and dramatic appeal to international visitors.

The famed Durbar Squares of Kathmandu Patan and Bhadgaon, numerous temples and stupas display half a century in building, is a fascinating combination of many architectural styles with craftmanship in wood, metal and stone. Stone carving or sculpture has also brought about its share of fine works in Nepal since ancient times. It has really accomplished the glory and grandeur of distinction along with other fine arts. The stone carvers turned many admirable products. The sculptural art of Nepal not only acted an important role in itself but also strived influence upon the art of neigbouring countries. Huan Chwang the Chinese traveller who travelled through Nepal in 637 A.D. and his travelogue about Nepal was full of admiration of the Nepali arts and crafts. Stone sculptures dating from the eleventh and twelevth centuries are more frequent which are almost religious comprising statues of gods and goddesses, mythical beings, stone pillars, stone-memorial are noticed steps bearing pretty carved animals are noticed as decorations to the temples and temple courtyard. Malla Period has produced an illustrious examples of stone sculptures like Royal bathings known as Shesnag, Sundarichowk Dhara, Tushahity Kaliyadaman which are reputed around the world for marvellous stone sculptures. Many exquisite stone images are found in all places of the country in temples and courtyard of shrines. Many Buddhist monasteries in different regions contain unique idols of Gods and Goddesses in stone exposing a rich religious feelings and cultural heritage. The architectural design of the Nepali Pagodas, shrines and monasteries that enshrine colossal bronze and stone images is an individualistic or exceptional feature of Nepal. The traditional shrines and stupas preserving images of stone sculptures add glory and grandeur to the artistic and cultural scene of Nepal.

Besides stone sculpture and bronze casting, another art form worth mentioning is wood carving. There are numerous intricate and beautiful window doors, temple roof-struts and other artifacts carved entirely by hand. These form of arts date back to the fourteenth century and the beginning of Malla period. Nepal is a land of unforgetable scene and historical as well as religious places, traditional artistry and the rich cultural heritage. It is enough to say here the expression of Daniel Wright M.A. M.D. (*History of Nepal*) as an illustration for the fascination of arts and wood carving—"The better class of buildings is elaborately ornamented with plaster and paintings, and the houses in general possess large projecting wooden windows or balconies which are richly carved. Some of the window represent a peacock with outspread tail; others contain groups of figures of gods; men, griffins, horses, birds, lizards, etc. and are surrounded by garlands of flowers." Actually, the age old Hindu and Buddhist paintings and carvings drawn out in the temple struts of Nepal with myriad designs from both Hindu and Buddhist religion, dragons, twisted lizards, cherubim with tails, lions, elephants, god and goddesses with many arms reflect intricacy and ordered pieces balancing a most beautiful art treasures. From time immomorable Nepali craftsmen are devoted in producing fine artistic creations, both for religious devotion and utility. The beauty of these crafts could be experienced while walking in three main cities—Kathmandu, Patan and Bhadgaon. Many writers express Kathmandu Valley as a living museum where fine wood carvings and metal crafts could be seen and sensed everywhere. The old Durbar Squares of Kathmandu, Patan and

Bhadgaon and the streets and all the inner parts of them have an alluring quality with their carved doorways, archways, through which one glimpses a courtyard and many idols decorated with flowers. The woodworks are picturesque beyond of any country, simply because of high level of arts and crafts is demonstrated by the finest and most delicate pieces of wood carving. Fascinating wood carvings are visible everywhere and represent some of the most beautiful in the world. The first matchless attraction in wood carving is fifty-five window palace of Bhaktapur or Bhadgaon which was built during the period of King Yaksha Malla (Yaksha) in 1427 A.D. and was afterwards remodelled by King Bhupatindra Malla in the seventeenth century. It is a masterpiece of wood carving set in the backs of the walls with gracious and sculptural description of 55 windows. The entire part is rich with the relics of its fabled past with styles, forms and designs in wood carving.

Kathmandu Valley's ancient cities and all areas in and around it provide opportunity for seeing temples, palaces of exquisite arts and designs and images of different gods and goddesses. Temple or religious shrines rarely stand alone but are a amalgamated into the neighbourhoods of artistic houses of local people. So consolidation of ancient cultural treasures like temples, stupas are noticed in monumental associations, both in urban and rural setting. Many other sites, monuments with art treasures in wood, metal, bronze stone are spread throughout the towns and villages all over the country holding many artistic facades amidst lovely natural environs. So Nepal can be called a land of cultural past which is reflected in many magnificent monuments, religious shrines and in all kinds of works of art. The rich arts and architectures of Nepal provide a vigorous and thriving tradition that has down unbroken through the ages. Arts in Nepal in any form, architecture, painting or carvings on stone and metal are at their best uniform and flowing. They are primarily rhythmical and plastic. They are spontaneous, elaborate in design and exhilarating. The conception and the overall design are wholly traditional but they are embellished with a daring richness of details and a delicate touch of workmanship. The affluence of its arts and crafts are expressed by the finest and most luminous pieces of bronze sculpturing, wood and stone carvings. They all have a distinct cultural identity and dramatic appeal to international visitors.

3

Festivals

Nepal is a land of many races and tribes. Its population forms of mix of different races, speaking different languages and dialects. They dress variously and put differing ornaments at different places. Hinduism and Buddhism are both equally honoured and the amalgam of the two religions into one vital entity has inspired and created the conspicuous culture of its own. The reflection of these exceptional character can be observed in the every day life of the people and in the works of arts and architectures as well as in the celebration of festivals. There are many castes and creeds but no rigidity. There is religious tolerance everywhere. Everything is based on compromise and understanding. So festivals are not merely spectacles for the Nepali people but glorious cultural heritage. Festivals unite together the Nepali people of different cultural background and beliefs into one nation. The numerous festivals of Hinduism and Buddhism as well as of other faiths are manifested in their own ways and these festivals are related to the gods and goddesses and they are celebrated on such conspicuous days as are consecrated for them by religion and tradition.

The people of Nepal are said to observe many festivals and traditional family ceremonies than there are days in a year. Nepal is therefore, appropriately called as the land of festivals. The Nepali calendar is dotted with a long list of festivals. They provide a glimpse on a fundamental insight into not only on religions but also the socio-cultural aspect as well since these gay and colourful events are also significant social functions to all people of all demoninations and faiths. Festivals of Nepal are focussed to present the national characteristic of its people and their religious tolerance. The Nepali year is an unending cycle of festivals which envolves the lives of the people and furnish them special events for family and social gatherings. There are colourful and appealing festivals practically every fortnight. Many religious celebrations, fairs and festivals are important means of social entertainment in Nepal. Vivid and colourful pageantry, lively and solemn ceremonials and the earnest warmth of feeling of a nation are gracefully manifested during the important national festivals of Nepal. Religion is the mainstay behind each and every festival as religion forms the life of the Nepali people from their birth. The festivals more or less are tied with the episodes from famous Hindu scriptures or Buddhist religious texts. Most of the Nepali festivals are related to the gods and goddesses and they are celebrated on such days as are consecrated for them by religion and tradition. Many more of them are observed in honour of the name such as, the festival of Matatertha, Gaijatra. There are yet others which are celebrated to observe the seasons or to mark the beginning or end of the agricultural cycle of the land. Some festivals are of national significance, such as Dasain or Tihar. Some of these festivals are confined to the Kathmandu Valley and, still there are others within one or two villages or cities. And yet there are some festivals which are only family affairs, confined within the household.

Nepal follows the lunar calendar. Different festivals are celebrated all the year round. The celebration of these festivals may be nation-wide, regional or just confined to the village or city. There are succession of festivals in all seasons and many of them religious in nature being related with one of the god of Hindu or Buddhist or of other religions. All festivals are commonly observed by the people and their grandeur and colourful costumes and procession are of great interest to the visitors. All festivals and annual events are connected with religion or with the customs of ancient Nepal. Many events have subjected a slight change through the ages, some uncertained their importance or some have been replaced with new ones, but these are quite a few which are still kept alive as pure heritage. All festivals are commonly observed by the people and their grandeur are of great interest to the visitors. Not affected with the stress and strain of modernization, the people observed the age-old festivals in their traditional ways. Nepal's festivals have an audio-visual union of unforgettable perfectness. They are demonstrated with wide variety of songs dances and music. They pass off colourful and showy costume parade. They are celebrated mostly in accordance with the changes of different seasons and most of them have a legendary origin. Some of these festivals are attended by performances of the classical masked dances which are lovable feature of the country's social and religious life. Many kinds of traditional musical instruments are played and they are seen in the different festivals.

The Nepali people are appraised as to observe more festivals than there are days in the year. Every day has some significance and it is celebrated with some feast observance, or pilgrimage. The people have to celebrated the birthdays of gods and national heroes. Nepal New Year usually falls on the second week of April in accordance with lunar calendar. During the new year, cities present a gay appearance. Greeting Cards are exchanged among each other. But the New Year mood is enhanced by the spectacular Lingo Jatra or the Bisket festival at Bhaktapur or Bhadgaon city. Coincidentaly, Thimi's Bal Kumari Jatra or festival also falls in this time and two of the country's colourful spring festivals that mark the Nepali New Year. The first month of Nepali New Year Baisakh heralds new hope of peace and prosperity and bring equal jubilation for all the countrymen. The Nepali New Year opens the chapter specially datewise for other festivals. There are most important festival of Nepal-Mahashiv Ratri is observed in February—March in honour of Lord Shiva—is celebrated at Karkat Sankranti which traces the end of summer and the beginning of winter. Thousands of people, comprising of persons, pilgrims from far end corner of the country as well as neighbouring country India visit to famous Hindu temple of God Shiva, Pasupatinath to pay homage and to do celebration of an all-night worship and vigil in honour of Lord Shiva. Likewise Nag Panchami represents the coming of winter. The festival (July-August) of Nag Panchami or celebration to worship the Naga (divine serpent). The serpent is regarded as the controller of rain and lord of fortunes. On commemoration of this festival, the main gate of every house whether be an office or private sketches of serpents are pasted and is worshipped offering milk and incense. It is considered that the serpent prevents the entry of evil in the house. All these offerings are bestowed to the serpent with the belief that no harm will be caused to any family member throughout the year. Another Festival known as Ghanta Karna points out the finish of paddy cultivation. Kathmandu Valley has many indigenous festivals as being the cultural and historical centre of the country. Ghanta Karna or Gathemungal is one of them and it is celebrated (June-July) in honour of the Victory over demon Ghantakarna. The name Ghantakarna means "the one with bells in ears" and the demon that has got bells in ears. The demon used to loster in the street of Kathmandu in ancient times by asking dues from pedestrians. Not proving dues to the demon would cause instantaneous death. The demon caused panic due to his hateful and dangerous action. To do away with such cruel demon, the people asked for assistance from a skilled Tantrist (occultist) and crushed to death to the evil demon with the help of incantations and magical powers. The festival is celebrated in victory of a mythical demon. The children of Kathmandu begin this festival collecting dues from all passerby. They exact a bamboo effigy of the demon Ghanta Karna in the main road crossing. At night, the effigy is carried and thrown on the side of the nearby river of the locality or burnt. There are other festivals of social importance as Matatirtha Shan or Mother's Day—children celebrate this festival by presenting sweets to their mothers, remember the mother already dead or gone and taking bath in the river Matatirtha near Thankot Village. This festival falls on the month of April. Likewise most of the following festivals are associated with divinities sacred either to Hindu or Buddhist mythology. Buddha Jayanti, birthday anniversary of Lord Buddha, is celebrated in the full-moon day of April-May. Nepal has been regarded as a sacred land by the Buddhist world since ancient times because it is the birthplace of Lord Gautam Buddha. So the Buddha's birthday is celebrated throughout the country with due reverence. This festival commemorates the Lord Buddha's three major events of his life, his birth, his achieving enlightenment and Nirvana—passing away into spiritual salvation. So Buddha Jayanti is celebrated as reverence to the enlightened Buddha and his teachings. Prayers are sung and worship is offered by the devotees in leading Buddhist shrines throughout the country including Lumbini in the Rupandehi district which is the birth-place of Lord Buddha, the Light of Asia. There is a great fair is held at Lumbini on this day. Hundreds of butter lamps illuminate the Swayambhu Stupa and the Boudhanath Stupa at Boudha. Another festival of importance is Krishnastami—the birthday of Lord Krishna falls on July-August. This festival is celebrated to mark the birthday of Lord Krishna, one of the incarnations of God Vishnu and the epic hero of Mahabharata. This is observed very impressively amidst colourful ceremony at Krishna temple in Patan and Changu Narain. People both men and women throng around Krishna temple, coming from far off countryside and commence dancing and singing songs in praise of Lord Krishna. The Courtyard of the temple ablaze with row of small lamps—Lord Krishna words to Arjuna in the *Bhagavad Gita,* the great Hindu text are regarded the very essence of Hinduism. The different places in the street are decorated with the Lord Krishna's picture showing the life and works of the God. Lord Krishna's idols are also taken around the country in different places in procession accompanying with musical plays and chants. The chariot of Lord Krishna is carried very impressively in Palpa and Tansen. Ram Nawami (January) is equally famous festival for the Hindus. The birthday anniversary of Ramchandra, son of King Dasarath of Ayodhya is celebrated with much solemnity. A great festival takes place at Janaki Mandir, Janakpur in Dhanusa district in East Terai of Nepal. Religious fast is observed and worship is offered to Rama throughout the Kingdom.

Teej or Rishi Panchami (August/September): This festival observed specially by women folk and lasts for three days. On the first day, women take a bath for purification of their bodies. The first day is known as Rishi Panchami and women wash their bodies with a holy leaves known as datiwan. After this women enjoy by taking varieties of foods including best of sweets and fruits. Third day is observed by fasting whole day and worshipping Gods and Goddesses. Jubilant crowds of women in their bright red colour saries visit to Pasupatinath temple fasting and bath in the Bagmati river, emulating Goddesses Parvati's devotion to her husband Shiva.

Chaitra Dasain (mid-March) is observed by worshipping Durga Bhawani and sacrificing of animals are offered. Chariot is carried and sacrifices are made in her temples amidst great rejoicing by singing and dancing. The festival of Janai Purnima or Raksha Bandhan in which Hindus wearing sacred threads or Janai take a ritual bath and give oblations to their ancestors. All high class Hindu males who observe the tradition put Janai (sacred threads) in their neck. These threads be on the neck and the threads are changed once a year on the festival of Janai Purnima after a ritual bath. Other castes, Hindu or Buddhists, who do not wear sacred threads by tradition, receive a piece of purified yellow strung on one's wrist by a Brahman priest. This is considered that by putting purified yellow strung on one's wrist will give power of protection to the wearer from evil.

People go to river banks for ritual bath or visit temples like Pasupatinath in Kathmandu or Kumbheswar in Patan. Those who are enthusiastic make a pilgrimage to Gosainkunda—the sacred take situated at an altitude of about 4,360 on in the side of Hangtang, north of Kathmandu. The special attraction of this festival is also on the popular stew of nine varieties of sprouted beans known as "quati".

All Viharas (Buddhist monastery enclaves) of Kathmandu and Patan make display of ancient images, relics many variety of tapestries, paintings etc. before the commencement of this festival and deserve a visit.

Pancha Dan occurs in July-August and on this day, the Buddhist priests go from house to house with their clean shaven heads asking for alm and chanting holy hymns from Buddhist scriptures. Many foodgrains are offered to the begging priests on this occassion. Traditional collection of artifacts are displayed in monasteries.

Gun-La—This festival (July-August) is known as festival of fasting, penance and prayer. Batches of people play drums, flutes and cymbals all over the city with recitation of prayers. Devotees sing hymns at the Swayambhu Stupa earning in the morning in honour of Lord Buddha. They spin the prayer wheels at the base of the stupa and offer their homage and prayers at numerous shrines surrounding the Swayambhu hill and way back to their homes. Buddhist scriptures and hymns are recited at Buddhist monasteries and shrines in the evening. This festival lasts for a month. The Mataya festival hold in Patan (July-August). This festival is a local Buddhist festival. A group of devotees playing musical instruments and dancing go around all the chaityas of the city from early morning till late afternoon. The devotees light various lamps is celebrating on the third day following Raksha Bandhan. The procession of devotees going to Buddhist Chaitya are also consisted of devil dancers and funny mask figures.

Then comes two great national festivals—Bada Dashami (October) and Tihar which are celebrated on a grand scale in Nepal. Bada Dashami—the grandest and the most important national festival of Nepal. The bright fortnight in the month of Ashwin (September-October) is the season for Dashami or Durga Puja. It is also the best harvest season in Nepal.

According to Hindu belief, Lord Rama conquered the demon King, Ravana of Lanka, on the day of Dashami, and therefore, this festival is popularly supposed to commemorate the victory of good over evil. This festival is observed by all government, educational and many non-government organisations and business houses, including the whole Hindu community for ten to fifteen days.

The first day of the celebration is called—"Ghatasthapana" which means the installation of a ceremonial water vessel symbolizing Shakti or energy of the mother goddess Durga. Sand is placed in a clay pot near the water vessel and barley seeds are sown. The pot is covered so that the seeds sprout into Jamaras in darkness. On this occasion people visit different holy shrines on river banks to take ritual morning baths. Then they visit temples of the nine important Durgas or goddesses to worship them. This is why the first nine nights of the festival are termed Navarati since each night is devoted to the worship of a mother-goddess. Festive mood pervades in towns and villages. Masked dances are performed in Patan. There is also a public performance of the Nava Durga dances. The festival of Pachali Bhairav is also celebrated and people pay homage to Goddess Ajima.

Five days (from the second day to the sixth) pass with normal celebrations. The afternoon of the 7th day in Kathmandu is celebrated with great pomp and show. This day is known as the *Fulpati Day* (bringing of sacred flowers). A grand procession begins at Jamal, Ranipokhari and marches towards Hanuman Dhoka, Durbar square, carrying a holy vessel containing a bunch of flowers brought from Gorkha, the ancestral home of the Shah Dynasty, Government employers in national dress join in the procession and it is very colourful sight to see and to photograph. There is also a large military parade in the Royal Military Pavilion, Tundikhel, in the presence of the King. A Volley of gun fires commences as a feu de jore in honour of the Durga Bhawani.

The eighth day is called Mahastami or Kalrati—literally meaning black night. Many goats and buffaloes are sacrificed in the shrines of Durga, the mother goddess. Such activities can be witnessed in the Taleju temple in the heart of the city inside Hanuman Dhoka, the old palace. The living Goddess, Kumari, being the incarnation of Taleju, is worshipped.

On the ninth day, popular as *Mahanavami*, sacrifices continue and people worship Durga Bhawani as usual. The tenth day, known as *Vijaya-Dashami*, is the last day of the festival and is concluded with the ceremonial application of the red "Tika" (rice grains mixed curd or yogurt and coloured red) on the forehead as a blessing. Four or five inches tall yellow Jamara (barley sprouts) are given with the tika and are worn on the hair on the day. These sprouts are gathered from the pot which is installed on the first day of the festival. Relatives visit the houses of their superiors to receive blessings on Vijaya Dashmi. Greeting cards are also exchanged along with wish of best of health and fortune. The Living Goddess receives women for tika on this occasion at Kumari Ghar, Kathmandu. People visit the Brahmayani temple in Bhaktapur to give offerings and to see the Nava Durga masks kept there specially for this occasion. Buddhists also celebrate Khadga Yatra through tantric rites in many places of the Kathmandu Valley. The procession of Khadga Yatra is another spectacular attraction. It starts after people come out of various bahals (courtyards) of Kathmandu with the daggers which represent the image of Mother Durga. There is also another phase of special interest during this festival which consists of the Khat Yatra (cart festival). The Khat Yatra starts from Annapurna temple in Asantole and the Ganesh temple at Maruhity tole. More illustrious spectacle is the Asta Matrika dance which takes place in the courtyard of the old Royal Palace in Patan.

Tihar 'the festival of lights' is also celebrated in the month of October-November, two weeks after Bada Dashain for five days. Laxmi, the consort of Vishnu and the goddess of wealth and good fortune is revereted during this festival. This festival is observed with gaiety and joy. Every house is washed, cleaned and decorated. People feel relaxed and happy and wear the best clothes. The near and dear ones of the family meet one another and those who are far from home return to unite with their kith and kin. This festival is also called Yama Panchak. A homage is paid to Yama, the god of death. Entire cities, towns, and villages are lit up beautiful illuminations in the evening for five days. Varieties of food including sweets of different kinds are prepared.

The first day of the festival is known as Kaag Tihar or "The day of the Crow." The Crow is honoured on this day as the winged messenger of Yama and the Hindu underworld. The crow is fed with dishes of good food and grains.

The second days is a day of the dogs. The dog is regarded as a gate-keeper of Yama and as a vehicle of the powerful and dreadful god, Bhairab. The veneration of dog on this day is considered the best way to allow an easier passage to the kingdom of Yama after death. All dogs are garlanded with flowers in their necks and given rich foods and red mark on their forehead.

The third day is known as Laxmi Puja. This is a day of the Cow which is greatly revered and respected in Hinduism. The afternoon and evening of this day are consecrated to Laxmi, the goddess of wealth. A lighted pathway is prepared from the main entrance of the house to illuminate the way for the visiting goddess of wealth right upto the proper room where worship is offered. The mark of her footprint is made as if the goddess had entered each and every room of the house.

The fourth day of the festival is named as Goverdhan Puja. This is related to Krishna who protected cowherds, cattle and farms from rain and excessive flood by providing them with shelter beneath Govardhan mountain which is raised with his little fingers. The bullock is also worship as a vehicle of Lord Shiva in Hindu religion.

For the Newar Community, this day is a day of the "Mha Puja" or the worship of one's own body in which the worshipper makes offering to God and prays to item for salvation.

Tne festivities of Tihar culminate on the fifth day which is the day for brothers and sisters and is popularly known as "Bhai Tika". Every sister worships her brothers on this occasion. The brothers sits down to receive Tika from the sisters. Yama, the god of death is evoked by the sisters. After this, a circle is made around the seat of the brother with mustard oil and water to prevent evil spirits from causing him harm at the auspicious moment of the Tika which is given him for his longevity and good health. The brother is then given a multi-coloured Tika on his forehead and worshipped with flowers and offerings. After this, the brother gives Tika to his sister. Many kinds of sweets, fruits and dried fruits are presented to the brother who offers his sisters cash in return. All the family members rejoice and celebrate the occasion with a joyful feast.

Thus the Tihar celebrations traditionally cover a five day activity with specific observation and are widely popular by the name of "Dipawali" or "Festival of Lights" all over the country.

Chhath—This colourful festival is observed in the Terai region all over South Nepal. It is observed on the sixth day following the festival of Laxmi Puja or Dipawali and celebrated to welcome autumn season. A two-day festival Chhath is celebrated by women with worship to sun God Surya. This festival is observed by fasts, prayers and singing hymns. This festival falls on September.

Bibaha Panchami Mela or festival falls on November-December. This festival makes the occasion of the marriage between Ram and Sita. Central characters of the Hindu epic, the Ramayana. A large number of devotees gather at Janakpur in Southern Nepal, the birth place of Sita. A traditional Hindu wedding ceremony is performed putting two idols in a chariot and followed by a large number of devotees dancing and singing accompanied by a concert.

The above described festivals are of social importance and there are other colourful festivals which are observed with great pomp and enthusiasm. One of the famous festival of such kind is known as Machhendra Nath (Both white or Red) Chariot festivals. The Chariot festival of white Machhendranath occurs in March-April in Kathmandu. A ceremony of holy ablation is conducted with traditional rites in the courtyard of the temple in Kel Tole in the centre of the busy market. A big chariot with a four wheel made of wood is prepared and decorated with tall spine of green leaves. The idol of Lord Machhendra Nath is put in the middle of decorated chariot which is dragged through the olden part of the city. Large number of devotees gather to pay homage to the God on this occasion.

Similarly, the chariot festival of Red Machhendra Nath takes place in Patan during the month of Baishakh. This festival lasts for a month and the image is taken back to Bungamati on an auspicious day after about a month.

The popular name of the deity as Bungadyo and small. The wheeled chariot is prepared at Pulchowk and dragged through the town of Patan in several spots till it reaches at Jawalakhel. The Machhendra Nath (Red) of Patan and Machhedenra Nath (White) of Kathmandu form part of the same cult of Abalokiteswar in the Mahayana Buddhist religion the month—long ride through the streets of Patan in his big chariot of Red Machhendra Nath ends on the festive day of Bhoto Jatra, the day when his sacred vest is displayed at Jawalakhel in presence of their Majesties the King and Queen amidst large people in festive moods.

Another colourful festival is named as Indra Jatra—the chariot festival of Royal Kumari or the Living Goddess (August-September).

This festival lasts for eight days. On the first day, a long wooden pole is erected before the ancient Royal Palace at Hanuman Dhoka, in order to propitiate the great God Indra "The God of Rain". Rain God Indra is very important for Nepali farmers because they depend on him for a better agricultural returns. They worship him for sufficient rains for good crop. So this festival is celebrated with great devotion. Classical dancers assemble wearing different kinds of masks and dance around the courtyard of Hanuman Dhoka in veneration to the visit of God Indra against the shade of gilded pagodas. On the third day of the festival, the Living Goddess is taken out in procession on a chariot. Three chariots of Kumari, Ganesh and Bhairav are dragged round the city for three days. The king also pays homage to her. During the festival, interesting dances of Mahakali, Mahalaxmi and Dashah Avatar (ten kinds of incarnations of Vishnu) are staged on the plinth of Narayan temple just opposite the Kumari temple. This festival marks the end of summer.

Another festival of Ghode Jatra (festival of Horses—March-April) is held in Kathmandu. Colourful sporting events with horse races take place at Tundikhel. Many deities are carried on man-borne chariot (Khats) in different parts of the city accompanied by traditional music. A demon called "Gurumumpa" is also propitiated in Tundikhel. The lovely chariots of Lumadi, Bhadrakali, Kànkeshwari and Bhairav are celebrated and carried in their khat at Asan. On this occasion, the Newars of the Kathmandu Valley celebrate Pasachare festival with great fun and fasting. The other aspect of the festival is enhanced by the grand function by the Royal Nepal Army at Tundikhel in the afternoon. Horse race and acrobatic shows are presented at this time in which His Majesty is present.

Sri Panchami or Basant Panchami (February). This festival is observed in honour of the coming of the spring season by worshipping Saraswati. The temples of Saraswati at Lele, Swayambhu Saraswati or Manju Shri is decorated with pomp and show. Large number of people visit the temple of Saraswati and take blessings.

At Hanuman Dhoka, His Majesty the King listens Basanta Rag (Spring song) in the midst of colourful ceremony attended by higher government officers and dignitaries escorted by mounted cavalier and a military band. Children are taught the first alphabet for the first time on this occasion.

The colourful festival of Holi (Festival of Colours—March-April) is celebrated by putting a three-tier umbrella tied on a bamboo pole decorated with numerous colourful flags is erected in front of Gaddhi Baithak (Throne Room) at

Basantpur, ancient Durbar Hanuman Dhoka. A great fun and frolic of sprinkling coloured waters and powders to each other. This festival ends after, eight day when the bamboo pole erected on the first day is pulled down and burnt.

Many other chariot festivals or cart festivals such as Chaitra Dasami (March-April) the dragging of Goddess Durga-Sweeta and Kala Bhairav is taken out and worship is offered to her. These festivals are religious in tone but more based on customs of the soil. These festivals are purely Nepali and are mixed up with the culture of the people. There is chance to see classical dances wearing different masks and the performances of their dances with typical Nepali musical instruments.

There are festivals which are observed in commemoration of ancestors living and dead and gone. One of such festival is Sorah Saradha—sixteen days of remembrance of family members who are dead.

Gokarna Aunshi or Father's Day—(August-September) The sons and daughter observe the occasion presenting to their father sweets, and other gifts. But the people whose fathers are dead and gone, remember the name of their father or ancestors and bathe in the Bagmati river at Gokarna.

The Gaijatra (July-August) or a cow festival, those whose family member have died during the year, send out persons disguised as cows. It is a carnival type of festival lasting eight days. Highlight of this festival is dancing, singing, making satire, parody, joke etc. It is a carnial type of festival. A throng of people roam along the street of Kathmandu, Patan, Bhadgaon, Pokhara, Tansen and Palpa Dankuta with persons decorated as cows. Making hilarious comments, mocking etc. are the order of the festival.

Guru Poornima (June-July) falls exactly before one month of Janai Poornima. On this occasion Guru or teacher is venerated on this day with the expression of great regards by presenting gifts and sweets.

With these festivals, there are procession of devotees going to a shrines or temples as Maghe Sankranti (January-February). It takes place on the first day of the month of Magha. On the day, sun reaches capricorn or Makar, the tenth sign of the Zodiac. From this day, the sun goes to uttarayana (North Course). It marks the turning point between winter and summer. The people in general bathe in the tributaries of river such as Narayani, Bagmati and Dolal Ghat, make worship and chant the hymns or bhajan. Trebani Mela at Butwal, on the bank of the river Tribeni at the trijunction of the river Narayani and its tributaries in the district of Nawal Parasi on the new moon day on the month of Magha. During the whole month of Magha (January-February) people bathe in the river Bagmati every morning and at the last day some of the bathers are carried in a procession from the bathing place to the temples. They carry water pots on their heads supported by bamboo strikes. Passerby take a few drops of water from them as blessings. During the month of Magha people bath in the river Salinadi.

Festival of Bala Chaturbasi (November-December). This festival takes place at Mrigasthali Hill, close to Pashupati Nath temple. Pilgrims make two and a one half mile walk around the hill offering "Satbiz" a mixture of seven cereals to countless holy sites and idols. It is believed that by making such pilgrimage the souls of their departed ancestors and relatives will have an easy access to heaven.

All Nepali festivals are of wide in importance. If considered locally, these are practically no days in the year on which there is not a festival somewhere in Nepal. Outside, Kathmandu Valley, there are many indegenious festivals celebrated by local people. Among them, is the most colourful festival of Khumbu region popular for impressive dance of masked Lamas celebrated at Thyangboche Monastery for a week with spectacular plays and dances known as Mani Rimdu festival, (November). This festival is based on the Tibetan calendar and is the time for merry-making for Sherpas from all parts of Solu Khumbu coming to the monastery. The courtyard of the monestery is packed with throngs of men, women and children. The ceremony begins in the first day mid afternoon with blowing of horns. The high Lama and a procession of monks enter the staging courtyard in their special roles. The the opening ceremony starts with a prayer and the people lean forward to receive Lama's blessings. The next day, the people, eager to view masked dances begin to assemble from early in the morning. A procession of monks enters playing cymbals, horns, flutes and conch shells. After a brief interlude, the monks withdraw and the masked dances commence. The musical instrument, Tenchun (a big trumpet) resound with deep bloom across the courtyard. The Gompa or Monastery situated in Thyangboche assumes a gay appearance with the coming of the first dancers clothed in colourful silken apparels wearing grotesque masks. The dances execute a systematic dance, exciting the assembled people, besetting from side to side, with weighty distinctness and heavy masks. The high Lama overlooks the assembly from his decorated throne. Gorgeous masked dances take place for three consecutive days at the monastery.

Dumji (July). Less important than Mani Rimdu festival, this festival is celebrated in all Sherpa Villages on the full moon day of the Asadh (June-July). Every Sherpa can take part in dancing and making fun and frolick which is not confirmed to the Lamas only.

Losar (February)—This is celebrated every year as Tibetan New Year's Day which falls on Parewa of Phalgoon (February). Sherpas perform their rhythmic dances followed by songs and dances in groups as Sheru and in 2 to 4 known as Nangding Solu. All Sherpa land is full of festive mood in this festival enjoying the feast for weeks. Famous Chhang, frermented home-brewed beer is offered during feasts in this festival.

Another picturesque and colourful festival of Pompo Yartung is observed in late summer up in the Himalayas across Annapurna. Many villages join together for an exciting day of horse racing and dancing.

There is another festival Toronal is observed by all Thakalis of the Thak (Khola Valley or the upper Kali Gandaki Valley north of Pokhara on March at the same time as of Holi. The highlight of the celebration is Taihsa Kyanla archery contest and the village people with great reforcing.

Next comes the birthday anniversaries of natural heroes i.e. Father of Nation, King Prithvi Narayan Shah birthday aniversary (January 11th). His birthday is celebrated as national Unity Day and a ceremony is held in front of his statue at Singha Durbar. He united all of Nepal into one nation. Tribhuwan's Jayanti—The Rastrya Prajatantra Diwas (National Democracy day (February 18 or 19). This day commemorates the advent of democracy in Nepal after the downfall of the one hundred and four years of autocratic family rule of the Ranas on the seventh of Phalgun 2007. The late King Tribhuvan (1906-1955 A.D.) ushered in in democracy in Nepal with the help and assistance of the people. So this day is marked with great rejoicing in colourful processions, pagentry, rallies and illumination at night. The nation also pays tribute to late King Tribhuvan Father of the Nation, in honour of his services to the country. Then Sambidhan Diwas (December) celebrates the proclamation of the 1962 National Constitution.

Birthday of His Majesty King Birendra (December). The official birthday of His Majesty King Birendra Bir Bikram Shah Dev, the present monarch. It is celebrated as a national holiday throughout the country. The event is observed by the illumination of public buildings, bonfires, parades and processions.

Lastly, Nepal has many regional or local fairs, and national festivals. In spite of these variety of national festivals, Nepal as a member of the world body—the United Nations and its several agencies observes and celebrates International days, events and festivities by managing special functions. Nepal observes United Nations Day, Human Rights Day, World Health Day, World Tourism Day, International Labour Day, International Children's Year, International Year of the Disabled, World Food Year, International Year of Peace and many more.

Anyone who visits Nepal from the latter part of August through October is sure to be surprised by the Important festivats to observe. These months specified above have got a successive of festivals all colourful and attractive. But the country has numerous festivals that line the annual calendar of Nepal which cause a welcome break in the daily works of the countryside. There is every occasion to observe a gorgeous display of costumes, fineries, rites and traditional musical instruments. So, Nepal's festival has an audio-visual impact of unforgettable dimension. The most important fact is that the spectacle that Nepal presents in her various festivals are such that they belong to a singular by themselves, so refreshingly different from elsewhere. Festivals are frequent and invariably attended by performance of the dancers in gay costumes followed by alluring music tones or by the classical masked dances in the case of religious dances and plays which are a popular feature of the country's social and religious life. Festivals or Jatra in Nepal are mostly observed in accordance with the changes of different seasons and most of them have a legendary origin. Festivals in Nepal presents prominently a lovely picture surpassing extraordinary tone and temper. The world's mountainous country presents the ultimate in music and dance.

4

Pilgrimage Tourism

Among the Mountains, I am the Himalaya—says Lord Krishna in *Bhagvad Gita* about the sanctity of Nepal as one of the holiest places on earth. The Himalaya, or the "abode of snow," is refered to as the early home of Lord Shiva and his consort, Parvati. The Himalaya has a particular impportant to the follower of Hinduism since time immemorial. The Mythological period covering the Satya, Treta and Dwapar Yugas, or ages, also contains numnerous references regarding the temples, shrines and holy places of the country. Many reflections are expressed in the ancient Hindu and Budddhist texts about the holiness of Nepal as the land of spiritial blessing and tranquility.

The book containing the rules of the language defines Nepal as " Ne Munina Palitam Nepalam", the land protected by sage Ne is Nepal. Many sages and seers preferred the serene environ and quiet natural atmosphere of Nepal as the best place for their meditation. To the Hindu, it is the holy land of Lord Pashupatinath. Many philosopher-saints like Viswamitra, Kapila, Yajnavalkya, Balmiki and Raja Janak found endless spiritual inspiration while penancing by the sacred banks of the Koshi, Gandaki and Karnali river or in the pristine Sagarmatha (Mt. Everest), Dhaulagiri and Annapurna moutains. Their in-depth observations and analysis of concrete phenomena regarding Hindu religiosity still dominate the intellectual arena. All these great thinkers attained perfection in their spirituality here. The hermitage of all of them was in the tranquil recesses of Nepal.

Nepal is the only Hindu Kingdom in the world. Religion is an integral part of Nepali life. Three main religious creeds namely, Hinduism, Buddhism and Tantricism prevail in Nepal. The Nepali people observe various forms of Hinduism such as Shaiva, Baishnava, Buddha, Sakta, Nath in both tantric and non-tantric forms. Shiva as well as Vishnu both have occupied a unique position in the religious belief of the people. There is a complex blending of Hinduism and Buddhism in Nepal and all the deities are worshipped by Hindus and Buddhists alike. An exemplary feature of Nepal is the religious homogeneity existing particularly between the Buddhist and Hindu communities, who, for centuries, have installed mutual regard and respect for one another.

Nepal is known as "Abode of God" since time immemorial. Himalaya or Kailasa itself is symbol of God Shiva, Parvati the daughter of Himalaya is the wife of God Shiva. Hinduism, as well we all know, is based on the Vedas, Upanishads and the Puranas. It has a basic trinity of three Gods, Brahma, the Creator, Vishnu the Preserver and Shiva, the Destroyer. Besides two of the Vishnu's other incarnations—Rama and Krishna, the heroes of Classic epics Ramayana and Mahabharat are also worshipped by the Hindus. Other deities like Ganesh, Bhairab etc are also revered. The Cult of Mother Goddess too, occupies a prominent place in Hindu pantheon. Ancient Hindu scriptures speak as said before highly of Nepal as being venerable place of repose and worship of Hindu Gods and Goddesses. So arduous religious sentiment urged people from neighbouring countries to visit Nepal on long pilgrimage to holy places of religious worship. Historical accounts refer that Hindus from India and the Chinese Buddhists travelled long distances to visit the holy shrine of Pashupati Nath in

Kathmandu and Lumbini, the Birthplace of Gautam Buddha in Nepal, enduring many hardships.

Nepal may be called the home of sacred places of pilgrimage full of sacrament and lively age-old culture and arts. The great religions of the East, Hinduism and Buddhism are worshipped by the people of Nepal in peace and harmony Shrines of both the religious Hinduism and Buddhism amiably stand side by side and have given a tradition of religious tolerance, which is quite amazing. The reflection of these uniqueness of Nepalese culture is still venerant. The holy shrines of Hinduism and Buddhism are visited annually by large number of pilgrims from India, Burma, China, Tibet, Sri Lanka and other countries of the world. Several pilgrims congregate to pay homage to the shrines of Lord Pashupatinath, Ram Janaki Temple, Buddhist Sacred Places of Pilgrimages and Lumbini during the Maha Shiva Ratri, Bibaha Panchami and Baisakhi Purnima days each year.

Religion is more than belief to the people of Nepal, it is more than otherwise a way of life innermostly rooted in cultural practice and social customs. Thus, the numerous places of pilgrimage in Kathmandu Valley belonging to both Hinduism and Buddhism and Buddhist Gods and Goddesses are equally venerated and these religious places comprise of temple of Guhyeswari, Buddhanilkanth, Machhendra Nath, Krishna Mandir, Nyatapola, Dattatreya, Changu Narain etc. Equally worshipped places of religion are also Swayambhunath, Boudha, Mahaboudha etc in Kathmandu. There are many other places of religious pilgrimage to both Hindu and Buddhist that lie outside Kathmandu Valley. The famous Hindu places of pilgrimage outside Kathmandu Valley are Janakpur, Muktinath, Barahchetra. Janakpur is an epic famed town and bithplace of Sita, wife of Ram, the hero of the epic Ramayana. The holy shrine of Muktinath on the northern shoulder of the Annapurna Himal in Mustang is an important place for Hindu and Buddhist pilgrimage. Further east in the Terai lies Barahchetra and the temple of Varaha Bhagavan which is an important site for Hindu pilgrimage. There also several Buddhist shrines outside Kathmandu Valley such as Namoubuddha and Lumbini. Namobuddha is situated on the hillock named as Gandhamala, 20 miles east of Kathmandu, a Chaitya containing the relics of Mahasattva is popular sacred place of pilgrimage for the Buddhists of Nepal and Tibet, autonomous region of the People's Republic of China. Lumbini, the nativity of Gautam Buddha is the most important shrine and a major pole of pilgrims from the Buddhist world. Lumbini lies in the southern places of Nepal in the Terai. A large-scale development programme is presently being taken for the conservation and the rehabitation of the important shrine, the plan will include pilgrims lodges, infrastructural improvements and landscaping and a tourist plant.

Holding the greatest religious significance, the national shrines of Lord Pashupatinath and Lumbini, birthplace of Gautam Buddha are sure to play a key role in future pilgrimage tourism. It is necessary now to make improvements to infrastructural and environmental developments and the creation of catering and service facilities for pilgrims, and tourists. Preservation of religious shrines and the provision for pilgrim facilities are regarded a cultural need, beyond economic impacts.

The prospects for pilgrimage tourism of Nepal are the greatest where cultural values such as the people, their religious shrines, historic monuments, and treasures and festivals are still a living culture. And whatever other attractions and their developments will remain the principal destination for cultural tourism in Nepal.

The planned development and preservation will help Nepal to attract pilgrims in both places of Hindu as well as Buddhist pilgrimage from all over the world and foster her socio-religious heritage.

Nepal can be called the home of sacred places of pilgrimage, full of religious curosities and lively ancient culture and arts. Nepal as referred in ancient holy texts may be called the place of numerous Hindu and Buddhist places of pilgrimage. Below is given a description along with the legendary accounts of Hindu and Buddhist pilgrimages. These places lie within and outside the Kathmandu.

The most revered and one of the sacred Hindu temples dedicated to Lord Shiva, is some 5 kilometres from the city and on the banks of the Bhagmati river. Pashupatinath is the holiest of all the shrines devoted to Lord Shiva, the guardian deity of Nepal, or the preserver of the universe. The temple of Pashupatinath is a three tiered pagoda of gold-gilt and brass of which the gateways are plated with silver. This is a sanctuary of the lingam of Pashupati Nath. A countless number of pilgrims pay homage to Lord Pashupatinath on the occasion of the annual festival of Shivaratri (Feb-March) when thousands of Shiva's devotees pour in the holy site from as far away as India and other parts of the world where Hindus stay.

Janakpur, birth-place of Sita, the wife of Rama of the famous Hindu epic Ramayana, is situated in the eastern Terai region of Nepal. It is a historic city dating back to the ancient times. Janakpur is also known as the land of the famed King Janak, who in himself was a remarkable store of knowledge and wisdom, and who also was the father of Sita. So Janakpur was the maternal home of Sita who got married with Rama, the virtuous hero of the Ramayana. This is one of the sacred places for Hindu devotees from India and other parts of the world as well. The temple of Janaki, built by queen Vrisha Bhanu of Indian state of Tikamgarh, is made of marble and is full of artistic designs and decorations. Near to the Janaki temple is another ancient shrine equally popular as the Temple of Rama. These two temples are thronged by millions of pilgrims during

Janakpur's two main festivals, one commemorating Sita's birthday and the other her wedding with Rama.

The importance of most the religious shrines outside the Kathmandu Valley usually lies in their religious and historic value rather than architectural or artistic featuers. But there are few exceptions such as the marble temple of Janaki at Janakpur, Gorakhnath temple at Gorkha and others. The all are in scenic setting with proximity to beautiful natural surroundings.

Muktinath: The holi shrine of Muktinath on the northern fringe of the Annapurna Himal in Mustang is an important holy place for Hindu and Buddhist pilgrims. This is situated on a high mountain ridge at an altitude of 3,749 metres in the vast rain- shadow of the Great Himalayas. The temple of Jwala Mai (the Goddess of flames) known as the chief deity and a female incarnation of Lord Vishnu, is housed in a small pagoda and is equally revered by Hindus and Buddhists alike. The temple is surrounded on three sides by a stone wall which contains hundred and eight bull heads, all made of brass. Sacred water pours from the mouth of these full heads. The temple of the eternal fire is supposed to signify the three vital elements, the earth, fire and water. To a Hindu, Muktinath is a place of piligrimage to achieve Mukti (liberation) which, according to Hindu belief, liberates him from the chain of re-birth. Salikgrams (smooth, round black stones) are found in liberal quantity on the banks and the river bed of the Kali Gandaki river which is proclaimed to be the emblem of Niranjan or Vishnu, one of the Trinity gods. The Saligrams thus are said to possess mystical powers. All pilgrims visiting Muktinath hardly forget to pick up few pieces of such smooth black stones. Many ascetics and learned sadhus can be seen traversing the rugged trail to Muktinath in quest of spiritual bliss at the place, being serene, automatically inspires spirituality in every pilgrim. The place is reached from Pokhara either through the 10-14 day trekking or air service up to Jomsom and a morning walk from there. To a Hindu, Muktinath symbolises of concrete phenomena regarding Hindu religiosity still dominate the intellectual arena. All these great thinkers attained perfection in their spirituality here. The hermitage of all of them was in the tranquil recesses of Nepal.

Gosainkunda—Another famous place of pilgrimage is a cluster of lakes of Gosainkunda, situated at an altitude of 4380 metres above sea level. It is located north west of Helambu and 132 kilometres north-east of Kathmandu. The Langtang Valley is situated north of Gosainkunda. It is approximately 18 kilometres north-east of Jomsom. Gasainkunda is a religious site in northern Nepal where Hindu pilgrims and nature-loving trekkers make a constant flow. The religious-minded visitors feel spiritual solace and are tempted to bathe in the first of a series of lakes in the month of July as they believe that Lord Shiva is supposed to be present there to bless them.

Swargadwari is situated in the western part of the district of Peuthan in Rapti zone and is one of the most famous places of Hindu pilgrimage. The holy place derives its name from a sage who devoted his life to meditation in the region. The sage, named Padma Giri, started the practice of Akanda Hom (Eternal Fire) on a holy altar nearby. Many pilgrims from different parts of Nepal and India come to pay homage every year on the occasion of Baisakhi Poornima and Kartik Poornima festivals there.

Gorkha is the place of the same fame. It has two famous temples of Goraknath and Kali and is the birth-place of the great unifier of modern Nepal, King Prithvi Narayan Shah. Gorkha also is the ancetral home of the Shah dynasty. Nath-sect has played an important role in the religious life of Nepal. The followers of this sect regard Machhendra Nath, Min Nath, Adinath, Gorkha Nath as patron deities with great reverence. The famous pilgrimage spot of Manakamana is very near from here. The temple of Manakamana was built in Pagoda style and it has two tier copper roofs. It enshrines Goddess Manakamana Mai. Now a cable car service to Manakamana makes the devotees to pay homage to the Goddess easily. The cable car links 3.1 km distance from Cheres (between Kunu and Mugling) at Chitwan. The cable car begins at the elevation of 260 m above the sea level and ends at 3,100 m high. It is considered to be the longest cable car service in Asia. The operation of cable-cars to Manakamana, one of the popular pilgrimage sites of Nepal is now reached easily and to give an opportunity to worship the Goddess of fulfilling the wishes which one wishes in his life. Proper care and preservation of this famous site require utmost attention of the Management with cooperation from local inhabitants.

Baraha Chhetra—Another equally revered place of Hindu pilgrimage is Baraha Chhetra. It is on the banks of the Koshi river, a few kilometers from the main city of Biratnagar. This holy place of pilgrimage lies at the confluence of two rivers—the Saptakoshi and Kokaha. There is also a temple of Baraha, the boar incarnation of Lord Vishnu. It is a historical place as the image of Baraha is regarded as the masterpiece of the twentieth century stone sculpture.

All these important places of religious pilgrimage are of special interest to Nepal visitors, specially tourists. Besides, Nepal has many other national shrines, places sacred to Buddists and Hindus. Keeping in new the archeological, historical and religious value of these pilgrimage places and their interdependent relations with Tourism—His Majesty's Government of Nepal has recently laid special emphasis on the preservation and promotion of such religious and historical sites outside the Kathmandu Valley.

The planned development of Lumbini is just one citation of the latest preservation drive. With all necessary provisions, these should be a perpetual process of preservation and restoration measures of all these religious heritage.

Despite the plans and programmes directed towards the preservation of cultural and religious heritage little has been achieved. As tourism is directly related of such important pilgrimage sites, tourist facilities in and around the sites determine their popularity which ultimately may contribute to better pilgrimage tourism.

Along with Hindu shrines and temples in Nepal there are many Buddhist shrines and stupas in Nepal. They are all described below:

Nepal the birthplace of Sakya Muni Buddha is one of the world's great centres of the Buddhist faith. Buddhism has its origin in the teaching of Sakya Muni Buddha, who was born in the Southern Terai of Nepal circa 563 B.C. Buddhist shrines and sites combine to represent it as the holy birthplace of the Lord of peace, non-violence and enlightenment. Likewise the capital city of Kathmandu has been equally renowned as a centre for Buddhism and Buddhist arts for thousands of years. Besides such famous shrines and stupas as Swayambhunath, Boudhanath, Namo Buddha, there are hundreds of Vihars (monasteries), Bahals (smaller monasteries) and many relics of Buddist theology.

SWAYAMBHUNATH

Swayambhunath is an old religious monument, a typical example of the stupa architecture. It is located on top of a hillock approximately 4 km. west of Kathmandu city amidst a lovely surrounding. Swayambhunath means "the self-borne word" and the stupas's great santity for the Buddhist of the Mahayana (the great vehicle) sect is due to the fact that once the Kathmandu Valley was a lake in the middle of which bloomed a lotus. And Swayambhunath nestled on the lotus flower. The stupa is a symbol of Mahayana Buddhism with a fifty feet high hemisphere representing the sublimity nirvana and enlightenment. This hemisphere is surrounded by a golden square projection which in turn is capped by a chudamani, conical canopy of gilded rings. From each of the four sides of the dome a pair of large painted eyes looked out at the world. These eyes represent the all-seeing eyes of the Buddha. There are five meditating Buddhas known a Akshobhya Ratna Sambhava, Amitabha and Amoghasiddhi. The courtyard of the Stupa contains many chaityas, shrines, sacked pillars and so on. There is also a pagoda temple of Harate, the guardian deity of the Valley's children of smallpox and other epidemics. Such as blend of Buddhist and Hindu divinities at one particular religious site reflects the unique religious harmony in Nepal. The stupa represents the essential unity of the Buddha and the Universe.

BOUDDHANATH

The Bouddhanath Stupa is a vertical hemisphere on a four-tiered plinth. It is located about 7 kms. northwest of Kathmandu city and is the largest Buddhist Stupa in the world. The hemisphere represents the word of wisdom which contains the relics of Kashyapa Buddha. It is built on an octagonal base and has about eighty small recesses each containing an image of Buddha. The Chudamani is composed of a steep pyramid. From the square base on the hemisphere, thirteen golden rings taper towards the upper while supporting a golden umbrella. All the four sides of the Stupa are decorated with the mystic eyes of the Buddha. The dome and its base are painted white and yellow flower petals to signify the lotus. The shape was renovated by the Lichhavi rulers in the 8th century A.D. From the very beginning it has remained a very important and holy pilgrimage spot for the followers of Buddhism, particularly for the Tibetan Buddhist. It nestles in the middle of a cluster of residential houses. The hemisphere dome has four small niches to accommodate the images of seated Buddha in various postures. Buddhanath feature strickingly colourful decorations which are a sign of the influence of the Lamaistic school regarded as the oldest centre of Buddhist pilgrimage, this stupa has numerous prayer-flags prayer wheels and religious articles in its surroundings.

NAMO BUDDHA

Namo Buddha is another Buddhist pilgrimage spot and is known as Namura. Located 30 kms south-east of the Kathmandu Valley in Kavre Palanchowk district, this is a famous stupa also known as the Dharma Dhatic Chaitya and is a venerated place to Mahayana Buddhist all over the world. It is believed that the Buddha paid a visit to Namo Buddha and venerated then Prince Mahasatva by bowing his head. This is where prince Mahasatva attained "Nirvana" and Buddhisattvas sacrificed himself by feeding his flesh to save a starving tigress and her cubs. This is artistically depicted on a stone slab nearby as part of the people's reverence to Bodhisattvas. Ths stupa of Dharma Dhatic Chaitya is encircled by many smaller stupas and the most conspicuous are the four stupas of the meditating Buddhas.

Patan, which means beautiful city, also known as Lalitpur, was built in 299 A.D. during the reign of Vera Deva. The Durbar Square of this city is treasure house of Buddhist monuments and artifacts. It lies about three miles south-east of Kathmandu City. There are four Buddhist Stupas in the four corners of the city giving it a monastic look. These stupas were built by Asoka, the Buddhist Emperor of India in 250 A.D. that was at a time when Buddhism was gradually spreading in the Valley of Kathmandu. Five minutes walk from the Durbar Square takes to a spacious courtyard with an exquisite three-storeyed pagoda-style shrine popularly known as golden temple devoted to Lord Buddha. Many Buddhist pilgrims pay visit to the golden image of Lord Buddha, and, as part of their homage, spin the prayer wheel placed on the pedestal of the upper part of the Vihara. The intricate decorative patterns give charms to the glorious sanctity of the shrine famous by the name of Hiranyavarna

Mahabihar. There is another old Buddhist monastery in the city, popular by the name of Rudra Varna Mahabihar. A temple near the monastery contains a fine image of Lord Buddha. The courtyard of the temple is like a gallery of different bronze and stone work.

One of the prominent factors that attracts visitors to this magnificent country, is her sacred places of pilgrimage of which about half the total number are places of Buddhist pilgrimage. Below is given a desciption about the famous places of Buddhist pilgrimage outside the Kathmandu Valley.

LUMBINI

For the teeming Buddhist millions from all over the world, Nepal, the land sanctified by the birth of Gautam, the Buddha, invoke eternal reverence. Lumbini, the birthplace of Gautam Buddha and one of the four major poles of Buddhist pilgrimage, is in Nepal and it has its glorious place in the world of Buddhist pilgrims. Lumbini lies in the south-west plain of Nepal in the Terai, where the Buddha was born to Maya Devi in 623 B.C. It is a sacred place for Buddhist all over the world. It stands on an equal footing with the holy places sacred to the world's other great religions. It is also a world's heritage sites. So it is attracting many pilgrims annually and will increasingly attract pilgrims from all parts of the world.

KOTIHAWA

This is the famous birth-place of the fourth of the human Buddha—Krukuchhanda Buddha. It lies four miles southwest of Taubhawa. Kotihawa is full of the ruins of ancient settlements, Stupas and the Asoka Pillar. To mark his visit to this Buddhist pilgrimage spot, Emporer Asoka of India erected the pillar and inscribed on it the story of Krukuchhanda Buddha's "Nirvana" and details of his own visit.

KAPILVASTU

Kapilvastu, the capital of the Sakya Kingdom where prince Siddhartha Gautam passed his 29 years, is associated with the Buddha and Buddhist faith. Gautam visited this city many times after attaining enlightenment. This city was devastated by the arming of King Virudhaka of Koshala during the lifetime of Lord Buddha. Two Chinese travellers Fu-Hsien and Huan Tsang visited Kapilvastu in 403 A.D. and in 636 A.D. respectively. Now this site of ancient city of Kapilvastu is identified only by archaeologists and historians in their search and research. This was testified only in the late 19th Century. The excavation conducted by the Archaeology Department of His Majesty's Government of Nepal amply proves that the present town Tilaurakot was indeed the ancient city of Kapilvastu.

NIGLIHAWA

It is situated four miles north of Tilaurakot and is identified with the ancient town of Solihawati which is considered to be the birth-place of Kanakmuni Buddha. Emperor Ashoka visited Niglihawa in 245 B.C. and consecrated the stupa of Kanakmuni Buddha. The emperor also exected a stone pillar and set an inscription on it. This stone pillar is still there lying to the west of a big reservoir locally known as Niglisagar. The Stupas, monasteries and other structures have, however, to be traced yet.

Besides these above mentioned Buddhist monuments and sites, there are other important Buddhist shrines and monasteries established all over the country. There are some famous Buddhist monasteries such as Thyangboche Monastery in the Everest region, Kyanjin Gompa beyond the Langtang Village, Buddhist Monastery at Braga in Manang and Kankesy Vihar in Surkhet in western Nepal. All these Buddhist monuments and sites scattered all over the country reflect an alive and thriving Buddhist tradition down the ages in the Himalayan country.

Buddhist beliefs and practices date back to Nepal since the time of its founder, Gautam the Buddha, who was born at Lumbini in West Nepal Terai. He was a prince who relinquished luxurious life in search of enlightenment. He preached the Eightfold Path of the liberation of human soul from worldly bondage and the endless wheel of existence.

In about 100 A.D. Buddhism split into schools of the Hinayana and Mahayana. Hinayana does not practice idolatry while Mahayana worships the idols of Buddha. The Nepalese Buddhists are the followers of Mahayana school.

The Mahayana Canon contains a larger proportion of the esoteric wisdom than any other religion and has always adhered more closely to the "Heart" as distinct from the "Eye" doctrine, the eternal life rather than the changing form of the Message.

Tantrism had greatly influenced Nepali Buddhism by creating the path of Vajrayana "the Path of the Thunderbolt". The main object used in Vajrayana Buddhist rituals is a small thunderbolt like scepter that is said to represent the infinite in three dimensions.

Buddhism, as it appears in Nepal belongs to third "School" which has often been called the third vehicle—Vajrayana or Lamaism, i.e., a school strongly influenced by Tantrism.

Lamaism, as the Buddhism of Tibet use to be called is a mixture of the best and worst of Buddhism and much that lies between. It is noble part of the Mahayana.

Tantricism's origin is found in the ancient worship of the Shiva-cult, the followers of Lord Shiva in Hindu religion, who is the destroyer and regenerator of all things.

Tantrism is practiced both by Hindus and Buddhists in Nepal. Tantra is so much important in the religious beliefs that Nepal has preserved rich materials for the study of Tantrism.

Tantrism welcomes all devotees irrespective of caste, creed, sex or wealth. Bhairava, who is regarded as manifestation of God Shiva, the Hindu God is equally worshipped by Hindus and Buddhists in Nepal. It unites Sakti, Shiva and Baishnava and known as Vajrayana as depicted above in Buddhist terminology and its influence is prevaded all the religious practices relating to various sects so, Nepal has been regarded as the land of Gods and Goddesses.

Nepal houses inumerable holy shrines of Hindu and Buddhist deities. Many of them are worshipped both by Hindus and Buddhists alike. This unique phenomenon is an astonshing complexity which can be traced in the beliefs of the people and in public festivities. The strange mixture of the two religions in temples, Hindus and Buddhist worship the same God and Goddesses under different names seem like a miracle that no one will be able to expound. So Nepal offers a vast subject of research and search into Buddhist literature and at the same time it offers an important study of the interaction of Buddhism and Hinduism as social systems. The correlation of two religions—Hinduism and Buddhism is quite astonishing in Nepal and their compromise is in reality the religion of Nepal. Religion in Nepal is an intricate and beautiful tapestry formed by the interweaving of Hinduism, Buddhism and other beliefs. Religious tolerance and harmony is perhaps a unique example in the world. There exists a profound sense of unity between the two religions while observing the fantastic anomalies of Hinduism and Buddhism in Nepal Mr John Sandy has righty put forward his views as follows in his book—*Monuments of the Kathmandu Valley* (UNESCO):

> "The Two main forms of Buddhism are that of Hinayana which was the earliest form and Mahayana Buddhism which developed from the former at about the begin-

> ning of the Christian era and was based more on the example of Buddha than on his specific statements. However, the form of Buddhism most practised by the Newars in the Kathmandu Valley is that of Vajrayana, an offshot of Mahayana and it is here that the philosophical thought of the two religions of Hinduism and Buddhism is very similar. Vajrayana contrasts with Mahayana in its emphasis on tantric religious symbolism but the two types do not differ in their basic beliefs."

Nepal houses innumerable holy shrines of Hindu and Buddhist deities. And Hindus and Buddhist from all parts of the world come to pay homage at Nepal's many places of pilgrimage. A large number of devotees of both the religions visit the temple of Pashupatinath, Janakpur, Gosainkunda, Boudhanath, Swayambhunath and Lumbini to pay homage each year. Similarly, many religious sites in and out of the Kathmandu Valley have served also as great attractions for international tourists. While some are beautiful and intricately-carved temples built by master builders of ancient times, other places are the centre of religious fairs and festivals. Many such religious sites be near a river or stream with the holy water of which the devotees undergo early morning ablutions.

5

Glory of Cultural Heritage

Cultural Tourism is characterised by a series of motivations such as the desire to learn and to study in a Centre renowned for its high standard of teaching, to study the habits, the institutions and the life of foreign peoples, to visit historical monuments (traces of past civilisations) or, on the contrary, the great modern achievements, the art galleries, the great religious Centres, to participate in art, festivals and celebrations, to take part in or assist at music, theatre, dance and folklore festivals.

Enriched by all kinds of scenic splendours from the Himalayas in the north to the Terai in the south, resplendent with historical monuments and artistic creations chiefly in the Kathmandu valley and other places in the Kingdom, solemnised by the tradition of religious tolerance between the Hinduism and Buddhism, ornamented by the individual and distinct culture, dress habits and social customs of the various ethnic groups and full of climatic variations, the kingdom of Nepal has within its short compass almost limitless tourist attractions.

Nepal is endowed with the historical and architectural aspects of interest. Among wealth of varied attractions are the historical buildings which are found in all parts of the country passed by tourist roads leading through the ancient tri-city of Kathmandu, Patān and Bhadgaon. The pagoda style of architecture is represented by ancient places such as palace complex of Kathmandu, Patan and Bhadgaon as well as by utilitarian buildings, residences, temples, stupas and shrines. Naturally of great significance are the well-preserved monuments which both in cities and towns are found in such numbers that sight-seeing tours are planned far-flung panorama. Culturally Kathmandu valley is the real tourist Center of the Kingdom. The arts and traditions of Nepal, inspired by ancient Buddhist and Hindu cultures, are of an astonishing richness specially in the Valley of Kathmandu.

Happily preserved from great migrations and invasion, Kathmandu with Patan and Bhadgaon, second and third towns in importance, constitutes a rare emsemble of an architecture of great originality and quality. A large number of temples (stupas and pagodas) and thousands of other interesting monuments and private houses (carved wooden windows) are within easy reach in the oval valley of less than 250 sq. miles. Some of these places (Hanuman Dhoka the old place in Kathmandu, Durbar Squares in Patan and Bhadgaon, the Buddhist stupas of Bodhanath and Swayambhunath, the famous Hindu temples of Pasupatinath, Taleju Bhawani etc. are now well-known and visited by the tourists and other places of interest like Sankhu, Chagunarain, pharping, Gokarna, deserve attention.

Many buildings testify Pagoda style of architecture and numerous predominant temples and shrines of the early Lichhavian and Malla periods stand in cities and are scattered throughout the countryside and are even found in villages. Many cities and towns still carry the typical features of their Mandap (ground plan), seen not only in their urban conception, but also in the number of beautiful preserved Malla palaces and buildings. Urban towns and villages of more or less historically important still have such a wealth of original Pagoda style that the visitor feels as if he has stepped into the middle ages. The historical and artistic standard of Lichhavi and Malla period not only document the excellent standard of architectural art in this part of Asia at that time (7th century A.D.-12th century A.D.) but is a priceless cultural contribution to the history of mankind. Similar testimony is given by monasteries, gateways, pavilions, and other edifices built also for enhancement of art. Most of the cities and towns consist of entire complexes covering scores of surroundings of few miles.

In the midst of apparent multiplicity of religious faiths and ritual practices, the most significant fact is that in actual everyday life the sects and denomination merge into one another to form one unified whole. All gods and goddesses command the deep veneration of all. Similarly, the festivals connected with this of that deity is joyously shared by all. Synthesis not antithesis, popularization not polarisation, heterodoxy not orthodoxy, is the main spring of the Nepalese way of life. Thus, it has given to the Nepalese culture firmness and grandeur.

Active handicraft, bronze and brass in Patan, pottery in Themi, woodcarving and painting testifies that the traditional taste is still living.

Naturally, relics of the classic period and of the following architectural trends of 16th Century are also present among the architectural pieces found in Nepal. It is better to point out that in Nepal all these architectural buildings are accompanied by combines and series of artistic works—paintings, sculptures from each respective period and are supplemented by objects of daily uses. Often palaces and temples house the complete equipment of artisan workshops and other production means of various bygone ages. Bhaktapur Art Gallery collections acquaint visitors with the wide range of masterpieces of paintings. There are also original collections of period clothing both civil, religious and theatrical costumes which can be seen in festival and other special special occasions. All these hisotorical relics represent an immense wealth of national tradition and are valuable tourist attractions.

There are many national cultural and religious centres outside Kathmandu Valley. The most famous are Janakpur—birth place of Sita and Lumbini—world famous birth place of Gautam Buddha. Janakpur is an epic famed town and birth-place of Sita—wife of Rama, the hero of the epic Ramayana. This place is famous for its marble temple of Janaki. Lumbini is the sacred Buddhist and the sacred Buddhist pilgrimage site. These two places of ancient cultural seats are very famous since time immemorial. We have a historical evidence that the Chinese and Japanese Buddhists travelled long distances to visit Lumbini—the birth-place and Pasupatinath temple, braving many hardships and severe endurances.

There are many Gompas (Budhist monasteries) in Helambu, Thyanboche and many other places which deserve visit to know the culture of the country.

So the cultural tourism of Nepal has a great part to play. In order to diversify the tourist traffic of Nepal, it is necessary to develop other destination areas in Nepal for the benefit of the foreign tourists as well as domestic tourists. This suggestion would serve a three fold purpse viz. (i) diversion of traffic from major areas (ii) strengthening of the infrastructure and (iii) exposure of the singularity of culture. In this connection a reference was also made to the recommendation made by the Master Plan on the development of tourism in Nepal which had selected number of places of tourist attractions and pilgrimage in Nepal for integrated development.

The Nepalese year is an unending cycle of festivals which enrich the lives of the people and provide them occasions for family and social get-together. The Nepalese people are said to observe more festivals and traditional family ceremonies from a birth of the child to a death of some family member than there are days in the year. Such days are naturally celebrated with feast, song, dance and pilgrimage. Religion is the mainstay behind each and every festival as religion forms the life of the Nepalese people from the their cradle. Hinduism and Buddhism are the two chief religions and the significance of Nepal rests in that the two have mixed inseparably. Hindu Gods and Buddhist deities are placed side by side. The people pay divine honors to both with the same reverence. So, the festivals are connected with episodes or admiration from the famous Hindu scripture or Buddhist mythology. All these festivals are celebrated somehow or other according to age-old tradition. Picturesque Pageantry, ceremonials both gay and solemn and the ardent ferver of a nation are elegantly display during the important national festivals of Nepal. These conspicous events are the heritages of an ancient culture.

Nepal is the meeting ground of the great Civilizations of Asia and as such she is the cultural museum where art treasures and monuments of historcial interest are preserved. The annals of the Chinese Tang dynasty contain several references to the people of Nepal and her art and living around the middle of the 7th century A.D. The spread of Tantric Vajrayana from the 7th-8th century onwards from Nepal to Tibet where it developed into Lamaism exerted an influence upon the Mongols from the 13th, and especially from the 16th century onwards Tibetan art developed out of Nepalese and Chinese elements. With the coming of Buddhism, the exchange of ideas between the neighbouring countries has taken place and is aptly remarked by Mr. Dietrich Seckel in his book *"Art of the World"* as follows:

> "In many instances it was only with the coming of Buddhism; only through the stimulus it provided and the aspirations it awakened, that are could develop fully and reach standards acceptable in all parts of Asia. Thanks to Buddhism the various art tradition,

> which until then had been largely regional in scope and self-sufficient, were enable to establish contact with one another on an ever-growing scale, to exchange ideals and to fertilize each other."

Chinese envoys who visited Nepal in Lichhavi era has given accounts of the rich prosperity and the high standard of art and architecture. By the description of the Chinese envoy, it is proved that the pagoda style was firstly evolved and developed in Nepal as he had not seen such architecture before. This style of architecture spread from Nepal to many other Asian countries in succession of times.

The cultural heritage of Nepal is undoubtedly unique. It will not be out of context to dwell on the problems of preservation of environment, cultural heritage and religious and historical monuments. But the way of living of the people is gradually coming under the direct influence of mechanised civilisation. Therefore, a question remains almost unanswered. How long can we preserve the way of living of our own kind? So is the case of the preservation of religious and historical monuments and sites. It is not out of place here to mention that to preserve the ancient monuments has become problem for Nepal. It is not because we have so many of them that it is almost impossible to preserve and maintain them. In order to solve such problems and to maintain the harmony of environment, which, in fact, is created by the world famous native architecture, His Majesty's Government of Nepal is at present preparing a Master Plan for the preservation of these monuments located at different places with the help of UNESCO and other friendly nations of the world.

It is the need of the hour for preparing the information about the culture of the country and its past glories. This is supported by the presentation of factual information with the aid of maps, notices, guides, labels in museum, clear and concise histories and sum-ups, publicity for the culture of the country through medium of brochures.

The unique cultural tradition stemming from and sustained by the harmonious blending of Hinduism and Buddhism, has proved a permanent source of inspiration for the artists of all ages as evidenced by the grandeur of the past along with countless other art products in wood, brass and stone. It has also inspired a calender of festivals whose dominant religious tones are expressed in terms of highly artistic symbolisms, popularly understood and interpreted. The reflection of this uniqueness of Nepalese culture can be seen in the everyday life of the people and in the works of arts and architectures.

Kathmandu city is for tradition, art and architecture. Nepal's capital city has many cultural treasures such as the famed Kathmandu Durbar Square, temples and Stupas, half a century in building, is a attractive combination of many architectural styles. Kathmandu Durbar Square is a complex of varied attractions for marvellous art and designs as well as for experiencing some of the greatest site of South Asia's cultural heritage.

Kathmandu Durbar Square, most popularly known by the name of Hanuman Dhoka Palace is famous as the most attractive part of Kathmandu, full of temples, palace buildings and courtyards constructed during Malla Period (12th to 18th century).

It contains traditional artistry and the rich cultural heritage of Nepal. The exoticism of historical remains consisting of palace buildings and temples in the Durbar Square offer elaborateness of artistic detail and beauty treatment which has no rival in Asia. Kathmandu's greater importance lies in the fact that it is the artistic as well as cultural capital of Nepal. Nepal by these singular beauty of art and architectural marvels is regarded as one of the few countries in the world where seven world Heritage Sites are situated within 20 kilometers of radius.

The second imposing cultural heritage is the Buddhist Stupa of Swayambhunath. This is regarded as a religious monument showing a typical example of the Stupa architecture. It is situated on top of a hillock three kms west of Kathmandu amidst a lovely and quite environ. This stupa holds a big sanctity for the Buddhists as well as the Hindus. The Stupa (Chaitya) is composed of solid hemisphere of brick and earth holding a lofty conical spire topped by a pinnacle of copper gilt forming the main structure. On the four-sided base of the spire are painted the all-seeing eyes of Lord Buddha. The Stupa quadrangle holds many miniature Stupas, Shrines, sacred pillars and so on. There is pagoda temple of Harati, the Hindu Goddess of smallpox and other epidemics. Such mingling of Buddhist and Hindu divinities is the usual and the unique feature of the Nepali culture. At the top of the stairway, there is a big Vajra or thunderbolt 1.5 metres long, a symbol of sacred power, lying upon a mandala, around the drum of which are engraved the symbols of the Tibetan calendar. It is the oldest Buddhist Shrine in the Kathmandu Valley and so it is listed in the world heritage list.

The third famous double-roofed pagoda temple of gold-gilt brass dedicated to God Pashupatinath is also listed in the world heritage list due to its superb architecture. This is the holiest of Hindu God Shiva shrines in Nepal. Lord Pashupatinath is the guardian deity of Nepal. The temple is a double-roofed pagoda. The doors of this temple are plated with silver. It is situated on the western bank of the Bagmati about five km north east of Kathmandu. It contains the lingam of Pashupatinath. This holy place is a mosaic of other temples and shrines surpassed by the colossal gilted statue of Nandi, the sacred bull, mount of Lord Shiva kneeling on a stone pedestal opposite the main.

The fourth cultural treasure of Nepal listed in the World Heritage List is Boudhanath Stupa. This stupa is eight kilometers east of Kathmandu and about two kilometers to the north of the temple of Lord Pashupatinath. This stupa is one of the largest Buddhist Chaitya in the world. The stupa is a hemisphere on a four-stage plinth. It is built on an octagonal base. The dome is set on a platform in the shape of a mandala and supports a beautiful proportional prinnacle. From the square base on the hemisphere thirteen golden rings taper towards and support an umbrella of polished metal. The four sides of the stupa are inset on four sides with the all-seeing eyes of Lord Buddha (Lord of wisdom) gazing in each direction. The dome and its base are abored white and coloured with yellow paint in the form of petals to signify the lotus. It has about eighty small recesses each bearing the image of Buddha. The wall around the Stupa is studded with the hundreds of prayer wheels that are spin by the devotees as they walk around the Stupa. The origin of the Stupa is a little obscure. However, it is considered to be built by Licchavi King Mana Dev in the fifth century A.D. Around the Stupa are various smaller shrines and the houses of important Lamas (Buddhist priests) and monasteries. The stupa assumes a gay solemn appearance at all Buddhist festivals when Buddhists visit from all over the country, India, Bhutan, Tibet etc. to take part in the sacred rituals.

The fifth cultural wealth of Nepal listed in the World Heritage List is Bhaktapur, also known as Bhadgaon is the home of medieval arts and architectures. According to a legend, this city is shaped like a conch shell (one of the emblems of the God Vishnu) and was founded by King Ananda Deva in 889 A.D. The city is located at an altitude of 1,402 meters. The urban city covers an area of 4 square miles. Pottery and weaving are its major traditional industries. The city lies fifteen kilometers to the east of Kathmandu and is linked by highway.

The glory of Bhadgaon or Bhaktapur is represented by the Durbar Square with number of shimmering pagodas decorated with exquisite figures and religious symbols. Actually, Durbar Square is the showpiece of architectural jumbles of the Kathmandu valley. It is a conglomeration of pagodas and shrines grouped around a fifty-five window palace of brick and wood. The square is one of the most charming architectural marvels and it highlights the ancient arts of Nepal. These showpieces are the Lion Gate, the Picture Gallery, the Golden Gate, the Statue of King Bhupatindra Malla, the Palace of 55 windows, the Bell of Barking Dogs, Batsala Temple, the Pashupatinath temple, Bhairabnath temple, Nyatapole temple, Dattatreya temple and many others. Among various temples on the Durbar Square courtyard, Vatsala temple, dedicated to Goddess Vatsala Devi with carved stone walls and pillars in Shikhara style, stands in the midst of the quadrangle. Then imposing temple of Taleju Bhavani at Taleju Chowk, built by Hari Singha Deva in 1324 A.D. is situated in the quardrangle with artistic golden spires and umbrellas in the roofs. There is also the Lion Gate bearing the images of Hanuman, Bhairav and Narasingha Narayan which is considered to be a lovely stone works.

Along with these temples and works of arts, the Palace of 55 windows is a magnificent palace built during the reign of King Bhupatindra Malla in the seventeenth century. Among the brick walls with their gracious setting and sculptured design is a balcony of 55 windows which is regarded as a master piece of wood carvings. Beyond the Durbar square to the Taulmadhi Tole, containing the famous NYATAPOLA temple which is an impressive five storey pagoda. This temple is set on a stepped platform of five plinths, erected at the time of King Bhupatindra Malla in 1708. The carvings to the arcaded pillars, windows and supporting roof struts are of exceptional beauty. There are figures of men, elephants, lions, and deities covering the stone staircase leading to the sanctum. Each pair of figures is supposed to be ten times stronger than the one immediately below. The eaves of the roofs are edged in numerous small wind bells. This is one of the tallest pagoda style temples in Kathmandu Valley and is famous for its massive structure and excellent workmanship. This temple is dedicated to a deity of the Tantric cult. Close to the Nyatapola temple is another temple of Bhairava (God of Destruction). Near by this temple there are attractive group of traditional houses and contain some very fine carved windows. This part of the city is covered with potters working at their wheels for making earthern pots.

This, there is another famous temple of Dattatreya built by King Yakshya Malla in 1427 A.D. from the trunk of a single tree. Wakupati Narayan temple is dedicated to Garud Narain. The small two-tiered temple set on a five stone-paved courtyard is wholly covered with metal. The doorways of embossed metal and the torana, the roof and the finials are all of gilded copper. Near the Dattatreya Temple is a monastery known as Pujari Math with exquisitely carved peacock windows. This was constructed by King Yakcchya Malla and latter repaired by the then priest Ram Dutt Giri. This monastery is full of artistic facades of windows. This monastery is world famous for lattice windows weaving carved peacocks, Bhaktapur city itself seems an architectural city. Works of arts with superb figures and religious symbols are heaped upon wonder in the city. The golden door is supersingly attractive, the pillar of Bhupatindra Malla breathtaking by its clean and fantastic beauty, wooden colonnades rich red in tone through carved gateways with emblems of God and Goddess upon their tops, and griffins of green stone drowse before many doorways. Above all, Nyatapola temple is admirable and appaling. The glory of Bhaktapur is represented by its rich cultural heritage, the affluence of its arts and crafts and, above all, its still-present antiquity.

The sixth cultural resource of Nepal included in the World Heritage List is Changu Narayan Temple. This is the oldest pagoda-style temple of the valley. It is one of the rare artistic heritage from the Lichhavi period. Changu is an ancient historical spot located at an altitude of about 153 m. above the level of the Kathmandu valley on a hillock overlooking beautiful countryside. It is considered to have been built by King Hari Datta Varma in 325 A.D. It is two-storied pagoda of the usual Nepali architecture with the chakra (Quoit) and shankha (Conchshell) of Lord Vishnu mounted on pillars to the left and right of the golden entrance to the shrine. The sanctum of the temple contains a bronze portraying Lokeshware mounted on Vishnu who stands on Garuda. The Garuda is shown carrying a snake coil is seated on a griffin. Every image carved in the wood or cut out of stone is so neatly, skilfully executed that every viewer is apt to stand spell bound. In courtyard, there are many master-art pieces in stone sculpture. Very beautiful and intricate ancient stone sculptures bearing images of Narasimha Narayan, Satya Narayan, Vishnu Roopa and many others are scattered in the quadrangle and just outside. Changu Narayan Temple provides a sense of rich history and culture of Nepal.

The seventh and the last is Patan Durbar Square which is listed in the World Heritage List. The ancient name of Patan is Lalitpur, meaning the city of beauty, and is about five kilometers southeast of Kathmandu. The whole Durbar Square is a cluster of pagoda temples and stone statues. Many pagoda temples dedicated to Lord Vishnu and Lord Shiva is scattered in the quadrangle which is one of the main city area of Patan. It is renowned for its awe-inspiring collection of towering pagodas and colonnaded temples of carved facades and stone monoliths having bronze statues. The Patan Durbar Square took its present form largely during the rule of Siddhi Nara Singha Malla and Shrinivasa Malla between 1660 and 1684 respectively. The Patan Durbar Complex also has devided into courtyards namely Mul chowk,

Sundari chowk, and Mani Keshab Narayan chowk. West part of courtyard is said to be designed as the residence quarter of royal family. The beautiful bathing tank and water-spout known as Tusa Hiti (Royal Bath) were built in the centre of the courtyard. Srinivasa Malla also erected a temple of great artistic design for the Agamdevta (Secret House Goddess) in the south-wing of the courtyard which is still guarded by the life-size figures of Ganga and Yamuna in gilded bronze. Over this shrine there is a three-tiered roof. The excellent metal doorway is indeed a tribute to the metal working. Adjacent to the Mul chowk and dominating the palace complex because of its size is the Deotale built by King Siddhinarasingha in 1641. It is five tiered and is dedicated to Taleju Bhawani. This is the crowning example of the whole structure around royal palace. The golden statue of King Yog Narendra Malla seated on high stone pillar is standing there praying to Goddess Taleju. The most striking temple at the edge of the Durbar Square is the unusual octagonal stone temple of Krishna built by King Siddhi Narsingha Malla in 1637. Scenes from great epics, the Mahabharat and Ramayan have been engraved around the lintels alove the colonnade.

The temple is of Shikara style and a bronze figure of Garuda, the mount of Lord Vishnu stands in from of it. This temple is an extraordinary example of stone architecture in Nepal. Near to Krishna Mandir, there are two other temples known as Bishwanath temple and Bhimsen Mandir. Returning to the upper end of the Durbar Square, there are interesting temples and shrines. The Durbar Square is full of temples with five bronze gateways, guardian deities and palace complex with wonderful carvings. This is known for its rich artistic heritage.

6

Tourism Development and Cultural Resources Conservation

Nepal is very rich in cultural resources. Dictionary often defines beauty as the quality or aggregate of qualities in person or thing that give pleasure to the senses or pleasurably exhalts the minds or spirit. The harmony or unity of all of the parts of a site or landscape observed by a person represents the structural or the scenic beauty of that place. Beautiful is defined as having qualities of beauty that excite sensuous or aesthetic pleasure.

People usually appreciate harmony and dislike disorder, friction and those things appear to be illogical. Scenic beauty as well as architectural grandeur both have many faces: majestic, serene, graceful, delicate, bold and picturesque. What about the opposite, ugliness? When we think of ugliness, these images often come to mind asymmetry, shapelessness, chaos, messiness and misproportion. Ugliness can be caused by the intrusion of one or more incompatible things into a scene while realizing the above discourses, it is pertinent that Nepal's cultural resources must be kept in survival for mankind's very inspiration and knowledge and for the long term sustenance of quality tourism. So Nepal needs to move now to conserve cultural resources before they pass being in complete disaster.

Cultural resources commonly refer a focus on the performing and visual arts. However, architecture, both historic and contemporary is a major into cultural tourism initiatives. The advent and success of city sightseeing tours in the tri-cities of Kathmandu Valley indicate a high level of tourist interest in art and architecture of Nepal. Kathmandu Valley contains beautiful architectures of marvellous designs and arts. They are famous as a vehicle for tourism. They represent a marketable enrichment of tourism initiatives.

Matching international interest in Nepali cultural resources with the existing but virtually unexplored opportunities for cultural tourism is clearly a major occasion to account for all. The necessary elements for successful international cultural tourism appear to be in place. Nepali cultural resources now enjoy international reputation as many international visitors have highly spoken about the elegance and loveliness of Nepali cultural treasures. Actually, Nepali arts and architecture embody the vibracy of national heritage and aspirations and represent strongest medium of nonverbal communication. Nepal has an abundance of significant cultural resources. Effective marketing programs can convert these marvellous tourism asset into a vehement market for tourism. Cultural resources can speed the achievement of tourism development objectives to the upkeepment of cultural resources along with the mutual benefits of the travel industry and the national economy.

Tri-cities of Kathmandu Valley set the standards for the excellence and diversity of Nepal's cultural resources. These cities are described as the open air museums. These cities are rich with numerous pagoda temples, stupas, monasteries and historical monuments. These cities constitute a rare ensemble of an architecture of great originality and quality. The arts and crafts of these cities, inspired by Hindi and Buddhist religion are of an astonishing richness. The arts and crafts of these cities specially in some of these places such as Hanuman Dhoka, the old palace square in Kathmandu,

Durbar Square in Patan and Bhadgaon, the Buddhist stupas of Bodhnath and Swayambhunath, Hindu temples like Chagunarain and Pashupatinath are well-known and other places of interest like Sankhu, Panauti Pharping, Kirtipur deserve attention for valuable store houses of architectural, historical and art collections of Nepali culture. Out of them, seven cultural resources are listed in the World Heritage List. These glorious arts and architectures of the tri-cities of the Kathmandu Valley give jest and intensity and a sense of identity of Nepali culture which form an important element for attracting international visitors.

There are many other places of cultural and religious importance outside Kathmandu Valley. Just to pin-point, Lumbini the birth-place of Gautam Buddha, the apostle of Buddhism and the venerated place of pilgrimage to all Buddhists from all over the world lies in Nepal and is also included in the World Heritage List. Likewise, Janakpur, the birth-place of Janaki or Sita, daughter of the King Janak and consort of Rama, hero of great epic Ramayana and place of pilgrimage to all Hindus from all over the world. There are many other temples, stupas, Gompas, monasteries and places of pilgrimages scattered all over the country, some in the mountain valleys and others in the lap of high Himmalayan regions. Nepal possess important shrines of Hinduism and Buddhism which are visited annually by great number of pilgrims from all over the country. Nepal has a tradition of religious tolerance.

Festivals provide cultural elements which create unique environment. The breadth and glamour of cultural activity make it one of the few elements potentially capable of converting into biggest attraction. The counterpoint of cultural activities can be helpful to attract international visitors. Nepal's cities as well as towns come alive with festivals in the streets, temples and monasteries. Festivals in Nepal are in reality, an open-air extravaganza embracing every form and style of visual and performing arts. During festivals, cities and towns fill with vitality and extraordinary tone and temper. Many festivals take place in areas of natural beauty with nearby recreational facilities as well as easy access to places of interest in other artistic, historical and temple yards. Dance, music, acrobatic arts and gestures are displayed during these festivals. These festivals commnunicate through emotion and visual perceptions and exist in their ability to transcend traditional barriers and stress the communality of human emotion and sensitivity. Therefore, targeting major cultural events and sites across Nepal provide a non-verbal map of the country, reducing the tensions imposed by language difficulties and stressing the anticipation of experiences to be shared. Cultural resouces and activities can induce a sense of comfort, familarities and focus into the process of discovering Nepal, its culture and the people. Nepal's rich tradition in dance and music offer insight into the focus on heritage. Music and art have no language barriers. The concept is no doubt poetic but also realistic. This reality and attracting human mind by music and dance have significant and rewarding implications for the travel industry.

Visiting local craftsmen performing their works which really supply the visitors the unique find in their visits. Performances of folk music and dance are staged for tourists. The multinational character of Nepal, its distinguishing ethnic and unique folklore give international visitors a variety of rich impressions and informative insights and a great appreciation of these national arts. A tourist attraction of Nepal constitutes everything created by man with an inherent interest. These include relics of the past such as architectural monuments of ancient age, pagoda temples, stupas and monasteries which provide an idea of the life of the ancient people. Side by side, another interesting objects man, his way of life, his customs, rituals, handicrafts, folk festivals, costumes, music etc. also are playing a pivotal role for enhancing the culture. Active handicrafts, bronze and brass in Patan, pottery in Thimi, wood carving and painting in Bhaktapur and carpet weaving in Nepal testify that the traditional taste is still living to enrich Nepali culture. Nepal provides an apportunity to explore a vast field of arts and archaelogy, enrich the sense of history and culture by fathoming a land with a religion and heritage.

Tourism development is growing very fast in Nepal. Influx of tourists continues to increase in quantity from the major tourist destinations of the world. Repercussions are noticed in the tourist areas of Nepal where more and more local population as well as tourists themselves are confronted with environmental problems. Pressure for growth and change is greatest in Kathmandu Valley and urban expasion have resulted more intrusions and a serious threat to the unique tourism resources.

The unbalanced concentration of population and infrastructural facilities to meet their needs by means of concrete structures of cement are causing growing concern and worries. The urban sprawl is now devouring the unique scenic as well as architectural splendours of the valley. "The Kathmandu Valley" as remarked by Mr. Amadon - Mahtar M'Bow, Director-General of UNESCO, "a miracle of fertility opens out amid the grandeur of a mountain landscape. Here survive the priceless testimonies of Nepalese cultural, expressing both the quest for an ideal and a remarkable history."

"Today, this unique composition is threatened with extinction."

Inevitably, intrusions into the ancient cultural areas of Kathmandu, Patan and Bhadgaon, tri-cities of Kathmandu Valley muddle a great menace to the unique tourist resources. They are endangering the cultural, historical and scenic wealth in the name of modernization. Historic core areas of the tri-cities of Kathmandu Valley are being shadowed by the buildings in concrete construction and stucco finish making the traditional texture of the historic monuments, religious temples and pagodas. Side by side with these factors, industrial establishments alarm to conflict with cultural and scenic values. Air pollution has been increasing due to vehicular traffic. A high degree of contamination of air has also been causing pollution with the concentration of industries and population. Shortage of water resources and waste dump clean-up are becoming a serious problem which ask for immediate attention. Not only Kathmandu Valley but all other tourist destinations all over the country are also facing with environment problems. Popular tourist areas, growth of tourism has saturated many traditional sites and has resulted in the rapid expansion of a tourist infrastructures at the expense of the environment. It is imperative that good tourism planning and management are needed now to prevent evironmental pollution with continued co-operation, interaction and implementation from a broad cross-section of the tourist industry. Environmentally sound tourism development concerns for conscious measures and activities which help the enhancement of the protection of the ecology. Restoration of a cultural religious and historical monuments is very difficult in Nepal. Nepal is very rich in these national resources and these are numerous historical monuments, palaces, private houses, temples and shrines form part of conservation. With continued pressure of use of these resources by urbanization and overuses the need to upkeep them becomes a difficult task—the big difficulty being lack of funds. These should be sound system of management established to make sure funds collected as fees at Heritage sites, should be determined to ensure that they are sufficient to meet the cost of conservation and upkeeps expenses of the sites. These fees collected at Heritage sites are used only as sacred funds for restoration and maintenance work at the site itself. By doing so, environmentally responsible tourism will succeed and becomes possible for the needs and aspirations of future international visitors as well as nationals.

It is known fact that conservation comes hard in the mountains and valleys of Nepal where survival comes first. Nepal is under-developed country and so its people are very poor. They have to remain in meagre agricultural resources. The people, specially of mountain regions depend on scare supply of foods. So being the case, the Travel and tourism industry need to act in two fronts, i.e. firstly Travel and Tourism industry leaders should act to persuade authorities to sites or regions where heritage sites are threatened to pool all energy to the conservation efforts. There is need for a large sum of monies for conservation efforts and difficult to meet out of national treasures. So there must be a provision of levying of visitor fees at heritage sites or allocating portion of trekking, rafting or mountaineering fees—all revenue earned by these activities and some appropriate portion of them must be dedicated to the conservation efforts of the sites. Secondly, there is system to be a drive to educate visitors that payment of a fee to entry into a heritage site payment is not a cost but an investment being made by each visitor for conservation of world heritage towards the future. Nepal has enveloped eight wonders of cultural heritage in its soil. UNESCO, World Heritage Committee designated eight cultural heritage of Nepal as world resources and so these heritage belong to all people of the world and must be conserved and preserved for all times to come for the enjoyment of humanity at large. Awareness among the local Nepali people is also necessary to solve environmental problems. The people are to be educated to promote awareness on the need to conserve the environment so as to give weight to conservation. The travel and tourism industry's concern, whether it may be government machineries or private or corporate sectors now on the need to give impetus for cultural conservation by heart and soul by educating the people with a sound scheme for sewage waste management, greening of urban areas, recycling of urban wastes into usuable products, to clean up rivers, the religious shrines, temples and pagodas and the courtyards of their own houses. Conservation of cultural heritages is possible only when local people are fully aware of the significance of these national treasures and consider these are their own properties. Conservation of ancient cultural heritage can not be executed by His Majesty's Government of Nepal alone, nor by travel and tourism industries but can be accomplished full with consorted and coordinated efforts of all plus the zeal and support of local population. Rousing awareness to local population provides alternatives to path of ultimate neglect of culture heritage sites and enhancement of tourism industry.

Realising the importance of cultural resources as a biggest asset for tourism, Nepal has given a great deal of attention to the conservation and preservation of these national treasures. His Majesty's Government of Nepal alone can not be able to preserve and restore all cultural resources of the country simply because of their large numbers and lack of financial constraints. Now work on conservation and preservation of cultural resources of Nepal are undertaken by His Majesty's Government of Nepal aided by contributions from the Federal Republic of Germany, France, Great Britain, Norway, Sweden, the Guide Foundation of New York, Japan and UNESCO. Nepal has now marching ahead to safeguard and unique cultural heritage of the country not only for its own nationals, but for the whole of mankind of the globe with international recognition of them in world heritage list.

7

A Land of Snow, Smile and Splendour

Nepal, the exotic country stands on the setting of majestic and glimmering Himalayas which remain one of the world's fascinating and exquisite natural wonders. Far away on the northern horizon, dominating the whole scene, rise the snow-clad peaks of Himalayas and in paralled to them a row of smaller mountains, tier upon tier, in bold relief against the clear blue sky, sloping down to the very edge of the Valleys. The terrain rises in sequence from tropical jungles in the south to Himalayan glacier valleys and peaks and the highest mountain in the World's Sagarmatha (Mount Everest), the roof of the world. Massive Himalayan peaks stretching across the northern frontier of the country traverse 800 kilometers of its central section and is known as the Nepal Himalayas. Here cluster more than 250 peaks that exceed 6,000 metres in height— a beautiful concentration of lofty dazzling summits. Of the twenty two lie on the Nepal Himalayas including eight of the World's fourteen highest mountains. The Nepal Himalayas of the north in their superb grandeur have the power to overwhelm the hearts of all who see them. Rugged Siwalik and Churia hill parallel to the Great Himalayas of the north seem to rise up all over the land.

The Himalayan range within Nepal fits in a geographical matrix as the culmination of a series of parallel ranges. The main Himalayas do not form ridges separated by deep gorges. Each of these mountain chains in turn sends out a maze of spurs dotted with numerous peaks. There are numerous valleys and deltas situated on the shadows of the Nepal Himalayas full of scenic wonders. To appreciate the magnitude and splendour of Nepal, one must visit over the valleys and far away on its own terms at its own—pace-trekking. To trek in the beautiful valleys and snowy mountains on its side, not only offers beautiful and lofty scene and scenery, but the chance to observe a simple way of life of people and their distinct culture. Nepal extends beyond the Himalayan range to the Trans-Himalayan area which is similiar of the barren Tibetan Platean. The highest and most dramatic peaks lie to the North and in the eastern half of Nepal. The dramatic complex of snowy peaks of Nepal Himalaya and varied topography forms the basis of the tourist attraction of Nepal. Set against the backdrop of the Nepal Himalayas lies a land of exceptional scenery and a fascinating people and culture. There is perpetual ice and snow above 4877m altitude in Nepal and so it is a land of snow and milk-white dazzle. The highest and mightiest Himalayan peaks are viewed as nature's marvel, vast in unchallenged and isolated supremacy. The panorama of snow capped peaks of Nepal is picturesque beyond of any country.

Nepal has enveloped spectacular landscape due to her world's highest lofty mountains—the Himalayas. Jagged white snow-capped peaks heading the sky, magnificent glaciers and mighty snow fed-rivers flowing through deep gorges provide singular beauty and exceptional landscape. The highest and mightest Himalayan snow peaks beckon as splendour of vast attractions. Northwards of Nepal at the series of white line of the snowy peaks of the central Himalayas, continued from the region of Mount Everest and Kanchanjunga in the east to Dhaulagiri in the west. The image of white dazzling peaks of Nepal Himalayas is of lasting nature which other countries can not rival in any way. Nepal, therefore, has developed tourism within this image of the Himalayan lustre and grandeur. The colossal

Himalayan peaks epitomize a charm of unbelievable beauty that is destination Nepal.

Nepal has a population of 20 million and one divided into numerous ethnic groups, speaking different languages and dialects. But all the people whatever their race or tribal stocks peacefully co-exist and this character or the Nepali people has created a unique Nepali culture. Proverbially, Nepali people are freedom loving, therefore they have never been subjected to external domination. The high snowy Nepal Himalayas have been helpful in the development of the ideas of freedom, adventure and romance. They are warm-hearted and hospitable. They are proud of thier tradition. Hinduism and Buddhism are both equally honoured in Nepal and the blending of the two religious into one entity have inspired and created the distinct culture of its own. The reflection of these uniqueness of Nepali culture can be seen in the every day of life of the people and in the works of arts and architectures. There are many castes and creeds but no rigidity. There is religious tolerance everywhere. Everything is based on compromise and understanding. So the Nepali people and their way of life act as a major attraction to visitors and represent an important facet to cultural tourism. Nepali warmth and friendliness towards visitors is part of their lofty magnitude of tolerance towards urban cultures and religions evolved through a long history of close contact with the people of neighbouring countries. Economically, the people of Nepal is not so rich but they are a happy breed of men, proud of their glorious past and sure of the great future that lies ahead of them. Due to their long tradition and glorious history, they are free from all kinds of inner stress. They have therefore, the broadest grin in the whole of Asia. Field Marshal Sir William Slim has aptly remarked or As has been well said by Field Marshal Sir William Slim, they have "The broadest grin in whole of Asia."

The people of Nepal represent a mix of northern and southern Asian cultures which have caused here to manifest unique culture patterns showing both the genuine roots of other cultures and their distinctively Nepali modifications. As we see that Nepal reckons with six major ethnic streams extending from people of Mongoloid stock and Tibeto-Burman origin to Indo-Aryan streams. But Nepal is really a veritable mosaic of ethnic groups and they are bound together by the ideas of peace, harmony and nationalism. Throughout the long history of diverse ethnic groups have preserved specific features in religion, economy, way of life and tradition which give variety to the national scene. The colourful diversity of the people of Nepal is exceeded only by the harmony in which the different ethnic groups co-exist. But regardless of their creed, religion or culture, they all have one thing in common—a friendliness and sense of hospitality. It is also said to the people of Nepal as men having ability to sing and dance even in catrastrophy. So the Nepali people are said to observe many festivals and traditional family ceremonies from a birth of the child to a death of some family member than there are days in the year. The Nepali people and their way of life act as a major attraction to visitors and provide an important facet to cultural tourism.

Nepal is equally famous as the land of splendour. It is a most colourful country with active blend of Asian cultures. An abundance of temples, stupas, monasteries and Palace complex specially of tri-cities of Kathmandu Valley makes the country a land of devotees who keep alive deep religious heritage. The beautiful scene of golden pagodas, temples, stupas, white edifices and red hamlets seen in a romantic background of hill and valley remain an uneffaceable memory. The prevalence of craftsmanship reflects the works of many craftsmen continuing their arts over the centuries.

And the way of life of people and festivals as common episodes dot the annual calendar of Nepal with all sorts of colourful procession and rejoicing.

The historical arts and architectures are the splendour of man made cultural values. Side by side with them, the wonderful flora and fauna of Nepal and natural attractions of peaceful valley add another splendours as natural values Nepal holds a unique place in the tourist maps of the world with cultural and natural splendours of god and man. It envelops nature's most secret colours, hidden away for ages in the spectral beauty of vast mountains deep beneath valley of wonders with snow-capped Himalayas, serene mountain chains, rolling green countrysides and the friendliest people everywhere.

Nepal is also botanically one of Asia's richest areas. Due to extreme variation in altitude, the country has from tropical to alpine climate. The climatic condition in Nepal is governed by its topographic extremities. The climate is as varied as and reflects the topographical and altitude bands of the country, from the tropical jungle of the Terai in the southern part, the hill region central hills to the alpine and barren snow covered Himalayan tracts. The varied climate displays a unique variety of geographical regions, embracing an exceptional scenic splendours. From the rofling flat land of the Terai, edging the foothills, up to the long chain of mountains enclosing lush valleys, through to the surging majectic heights of the Himalayas, Nepal offers within her small area such a huge variety of everything that it is perfectly tailored to meet the interest of every type of visitors. The tropical Terai lowlands possess a wide range of wildlife—elephant, rhinoceros, wild buffalo, tiger, leopard , bear, boar, deer and monkeys. The mid-hill regions are less in wildlife. The lower parts of the Himalayas house the Himalayan bear, serow, goral, thar and Nepal's national bird 'Daffe' pheasant while the unhabited valleys of the Himalayas shelter many rare species of wildlife such as blue sheep, red panda, snow leopard and musk deer. Variety of splendour is the true delight of Himalayan travel.

Nepal is also a nature's playground, it has tropical, subtropical to alpine type of vegetation, sal and sissom, Acacea grow in abundance. Inner Terai, Savannah forests are full of tall grasses and bamboo. In the middle Himalayan zone or the hill country, the climate is temperate and pines, rhododendrones, elms, poplars, walnuts and willow shoot up in plenty. In the higher Himalayan region—oaks, maples and pines spread in attractive setting. Alpine zone covers with jumpers, short rhododendrous and varieties of medicinal herbs. Rhododendrous with flavouring colour, her national flower are in profusion on hillsides. Eidelweiss graces the fringes of her highest valley in the Himalaya. It is a country of panorama of changing scenery, the rugged mountains the timbered slopes of the wide sweeps of river beds, the deepest gorges, glacier morains, water falls, picturesque lakes, resplandent lush green valleys. Natural splendour in Nepal unfolds delights and thrills amidst natural wonderland.

8

Adventure Tourism—Big Potential

Natural panorama and beauty of the natural surrounding are considered the raw material for tourism. Due to its physiographical frame, Nepal unfolds natural and scenic attraction of singular diffusion extending from the tropical forest belt in the south to the lofty alpine regions and the barren landscape of the plateau, intervening these limits spread areas plenty of outermost scenic landscape fastening a sumptuous diversified possession of recreational resources. It is this usual feature which forms some of earth's most impressive tourist attractions. The sublime mountain loops of the Himalayas are an enticement not only for world's alpinists but also exhibit an important asset to recreational use and an essential facet for cultural tourism.

Wildlife resources of the Terai plains and in the various regions of the country represent potential suitable for adventure tourims. A rich wild life and other valuable assets to recreational use are the country's natural forests, snowfed rivers and lakes providing recreational activities such as white water rafting, fishing, boating and wild-life watching.

The prospects for adventurre tourism are greatest in Nepal where altitude, topography and climate stipulate ideal pre-requisites for such activities. Nepal has got four valuable assets for the development of adventure tourism and these are pointed out in the following way:

The foremost and eminent resource of adventure tourism in Nepal is mountaineering. The Himalayas constitute one of the noble features of the Nepali landscape. The Himlalyan chain is an inspiring wonder of snow-covered summits, lofty cliffs, outrageous glaciers, zigzag rivers and deep and narrow gorges. The Himalayas of Nepal are the loftiest mountain ranges in the world and include the world's highest peaks. They constitute the dominant part of the great arch of the Himalayas. From East to West Nepal, the Himalayas compose of an exceedingly greatest mass of mountains having more than 7,600 meters, topped by 8848 meters Mount Everest, the highest peak in the world together with some eight snow peaks of over 8000 meters and about two hundred 4877 meters peaks. The Himalayan chains like the Kumbhakarna, the Jugal and the Machhapuchhre fan out from the east to the west. In this region, the world's famous peaks of Mount Everest (8848m), Kanchanjugha (8585m) Makalu (8501m), Dhaulagiri (8167m) and Annapurna (8091m) are located. Due to these row of mountain of peaks of different sizes and dimensions, Nepal Himalayas are of exceptional attraction for the mountaineers. There is nothing to excel or compete the serenity of these lofty peaks and episodic drama of their glaciers. The first endeavour to climb Sagarmatha (Mt. Everest), the highest peak in the world, was made as early as 1922 A.D. The Nepal Himalaya have since become a great centre of mountaineering activities. For all keen adventurers who like to show their feats, the Nepal Himalaya is always attractive and challenging. The Nepal Himalaya has thus encased and attested many achievements and tragedies in the last decades. They make up a remarkable chapter in human endeavour. Nepal offers one of the unique itineraries for the alpinists all the world over as a part of adventure tourism. For adventurers, there is nothing more than a lure of the Nepal Himalaya.

Trekking tourism is another part of adventure tourism in Nepal. Trekking activities are becoming more and more popular in Nepal and are recording a gradual increase over the last few years. Trekking indulges an uninterrupted and closest scenario of the snowy summits of number of highest peaks in the Himalayas, narrow-crested hills in knots, trackless crests and placated ravines, narrow valleys with people and their gay festivals and ceremonies. Unlike mountaineering expeditions, trekking can be undertaken by any adventurer who simply seeks a retiring experience from the madding hub of the city. Nepal has in great plenty of all kinds of trekking possibilities from arduous trek which may ascend about 6,630 meters to shorter at lesser altitudes around the mountain rim of the valley. Nepal's enigma and natural beauty draw out travellers from all over the world, who come to experience for themselves Nepal's uniqueness as a trekking destination. Some of the most popular trails are the trek to the Mt. Everest base camp, Pokhara to Jomsom, Langtang, Ganesh Himal, Kanchanjungha Himal and Khumbu Himal trails. Nepal stands out as the world's most popular country for trekkers and adaventure tourists in general. Beneath the Nepal's hill country where the most of the important trekking routes are situated. Life of the smiling and hospitable people in these areas have been little touched by the cross-current of modern civilization and so remain completely unspoilt. Trekking is the only way to really see and appreciate the country. Due to these factors, the general trend towards the wider development and increased popularity of 'Adventure' tourism within Asia over recent years, has been the boom of trekking in Nepal.

Rafting in Nepal's major rivers has become gaining popular with adventurers as it is one more means of enjoying countryside and ethnic life-style while experiencing the thrill of adventure. At present, the three most commonly rafted rivers are the Sun Kosi, the Trisuli and the Seti and there are other more turbulent and challenging rivers. Narrow-crested rivers strung together as a tangle in coils, dovetailing and twisting, pushing and plunging create breath taking adventure. River rafting in Nepal in the eerie depth of the deepest gorge in the world cut by tectonic snow-fed rivers flowing through the bank of ageless enchantments of the picturesque valley, offers exciting journey for adventuresome, a unique opportunity to experience a fantasy unbelievable realm that is destination Nepal.

Nepal's physical site and character are considered as unique and spectacular. Nepal is nature's playground and a paradise for Nature lovers. She has a magnetic attraction for nature lovers due to its tropical, sub-tropical and alpine climates with such natural differences on its flora and fauna within its small compass.

The adventurer or the natural lover can arrange Safari tour to the Terai tropical jungle on the elephant's back to observe a sudden rush of one-horned rhinos and stalking tigers. The adventurers have a choice of adventure which consist of Safari tours in the tropical areas as well as alpine regions. The tropical areas include tiger, the great one-horned rhinocerous, the leopard, Gaur, wild buffalo, Asian elephant, sloth bear, wild bear, sambar deer, spotted deer, hog deer, barking deer, wild dog, jackal, civat cat, fishing cat, bear, mongoose, otter, dolphin, crocodile and over 400 identified bird species. Sub-tropical areas house tiger, leopard, wild boar, crocodile, cheetal and other animals and birds. Alpine regions abound with musk deer, Himalayan Thar etc. There are many National Parks and wild life reserves for viewing wild life in their natural habitat. The famous National Parks are Royal Chitwan National Park, Langtang National Park, Lake Rara National Park. The wild life reserves are Sukla Phanta wild life reserve, Karnali wild life reserve, Shey wild life reserve, Koshi Tappu wild life reserve etc. All these areas are preserved for nature conservation and so it is prohibited to shot with guns but the visitor can shot with the electronic click of his camera.

All operations for adventure tourism are manned and managed by the licensed travel and trekking agencies who sell, rent and arrange everything a visitor needs. The agencies not only provide the most up-to date equipments but also can arrange transportation, guides and the meals to be enjoyed. Nepal is a holiday Kingdom with a series of adventure tours with different duration and thrill adding a dimension of depth in tingle of sense or emotion and acquaintance with long and varied observation. They can also supplement demand for package deal combining trekking plus mountaineering, trekking combined with white-water rafting and wild life safari which makes use of adventure parts of the potential on offer.

Nepal is a land unique in many ways. Despite the small size of the country, it has an astonishing diversity of culture and natural attractions. Nepal's variegated picturesque panorama and its mystical charm has been attracting people since it opened its door for international visitors. The different topography of the country provides it with a wide variety of climatic conditions, varying from the freezing cold of the Himalayan zone to the warm heat of the southern Terai, the midland hills and green valleys between them have a soothing climate.

Nepal is a source of perennial lure for the inquisitive, bold and adventurer. Many visitors who have travelled, narrated it as a destination of many different ethnic people with hospitable traits, many animals. birds, flowers, many cultural activities with distinct customs and traditions, collection of magnificent arts and architecture, unspoilt natural beauties and attractions. Being situated in the Trans-Asian route, it is a destination of a unique and charming tourism potentials characteristic of its own, quite different from other tourist destination of the world.

The temperature, climate and rainfall of Nepal differ from place to place. Terai, the southern region has tropical hot climate all the year. The central mountain region has a sub-tropical cool climate. The northern Great Himalayan

Region has an alpine climate. Due to these climatic variations, Nepal abounds in an opportunity for adventure. The energetic visitor could trek from Jiri to the Mt. Everest base camp, going all the footsteps of rugged mountains or circle the Annapurna Range. If a visitor has limited time and breath, there is still easy to arrange an adventurous trip. Royal Nepal Airlines and other private airlines can organise or can drop the visitor off in the middle of Everest Region or just down the mountain and the valley from the shrine of Muktinath behind Annapurna or at the base of the rhino-filled jungle. On a rafting adventure, the bold visitor can float calmly through the forest-clad hills and pass foaming rapids, sound and safe.

The newest adventure is the mountain biking in Nepal. The visitor can ride bicycle and go out to explore the view sites, the temples and the highways, Kathmandu valley and beyond.

There is no dearth of thing to do in Nepal for the adventurous or energetic. There is long trek or Jungle safari and white-water rafting in the trubulent water bodies of the snowy rivers. To more arduous and adventure, there is mountain climbing of various heights and dimension. The relaxed visitor can combine nature and culture with mountain viewing from a variety of look-out points and historical towns throughout Nepal.

Adventure tourism has a big potential for Nepal due to remoteness and inaccessibility apart from inhospitable and often forbidding nature. These characteristics have preserved large areas of unique wildeness in Nepal provide a potential for recreational use. Adventure travel can be enjoyed in Nepal due to inherent potential it holds. The anticipated trend towards activity oriented vacation, mountain recreation in the Himalayas can supply an alternative form of this type of holiday which is today on sea side recreation. A Nepal adventure travel is able to offer everything that is indeterminate group expects of a sporting recreative and cultural holiday. There is choice of adventure in Nepal which consist of trekking in the mountain terrain for a week or even for a month by trekking up to the Everest base camp. For the more adventurous visitor, there is white-water rafting in the fast flowing rivers of the glacial waters of the various rivers of Nepal. White-water rafting has become another major type of sporting tourism in Nepal. Rafting trips are of varying duration and usually take place on such rivers as the Trisuli, Narayani, Marshyangdi, Seti, Kaligandaki and Sunkosi. Rafting trips can be scenic float-trips down the smooth and shallow rivers or more adventurous "white-water" rafting where one has to shoot the rapids. Many rafting agencies now organize "Combination trips" consisting of trekking and rafting or alternatively a rafting trip down to Trisuli river to Royal Chitwan National Park for wildlife viewing. Nepal's tropical and alpine forests shelter numerous species of wild animals.

Nepal has National Parks and Wildlife Reserves in the tropical as well as alpine regions. The tropical forests are rich in species of wild animals including one-horned rhinos, wild elephants, tigers and leopards, crocodiles and monkeys. Similarly, alpine regions shelter the Tibetan hare, Himalayan weasel, snow leopard, goral, serow, Himalayan black bear, musk and barking deer and variety of birds including pheasants and partridges. These parks and reserves offer plenty of opportunity to view wildlife from close angles.

White water rafting has a charm and attraction in Nepal. Nepal is transversed by many snow-fed rivers. There are few countries in the world that are susceptible of competing with the exiciting variety of river trips available in Nepal. So the energetic entrepreneurs of Nepal have been organising adventurous spot tourism sightseeing via river trips. White water rafting makes it possible to experience not only to view majestic snow-capped Himalayas but also to see the flora, fauna, and unique rural life of the surrounding areas along the banks of the trubulent rivers. It provides an opportunity to observe many of the cultural activities as well as a fun and adventurous way to experience the joys of outdoor life.

Trekking has become synonomous with Nepal. Trekking in the Himalayan slopes up to the altitude of 5,000 m is within the scope of the visitor and has developed as a major sport tourism. Trekking tourism is the mainstay of Nepal Tourism. The famous trekking areas are divided into the following:

— Visitors favour the area of greatest fame (Mt. Everest region) or most dramatic scenery (Jomsom).

— Trekking is generally popular in more easily accessible regions with cheap and convenient access i.e. Everest, Pokhara, Helambu, Gosaikund and Langtang.

Some areas of the Himalayas are known for classic trekking such as Muktinath, Manang, Mustang Lamjung, Jumla, Rara etc. To trek in these areas the visitor must be adventurous, strong and stout.

The trek will reveal picturesque villages, rich varied of flora and fauna, viewing the highest Himalayan peaks in the world and the typical life style of the people and their festivals. Trekking, in fact, is the sporting tourism as the visitor walks on foot which is the only way of really knowing the people and places intimately. Nepal has the natural product for trekking and her people are the friendliest.

Trekking track consists mainly of mountainous way with steep up and downs. The romance of Nepal can be enjoyed walking down the rough and steep mountain trails down a suspension bridge and this activity is surely be a good sporting activity. Trekking is really the visitor's sporting pastime which provides variety of views from the safe landscapes that rise from the valleys to the towering peaks of the Himalayas.

Nepal is among the most fascinating regions of the world for adventures. It is a magnificent country with a rich and beautiful cultural and natural heritage. Nepal Himalaya is the challenge for adventures. The towering Himalayas stand awesome and majestic with their snow-capped peaks as an open challenge to adventurers, mountaineers and explorers from around the world. Nepal Himalayas represent one of the majestic features of the Nepalese landscape. Eight of the world's fourteen peaks all exceeding 8,000 meters are in Nepal—Sagarmatha (Mt. Everest) the tallest mountain in the world, Kanchanjunga, Lhotse, Makalu, Dhaulagiri, Manslau, Cho-ouou and Annapurna. These Himalayan peaks and their towering miracles are always becoming the climbing aspiration to the mountaineers are tempered to scale these mountains as French mountaineer Lionel Terray called it the "Conquest of the useless". Similiarly, George Leigh Mallory said in a characterstic British tone "because it's there."

Whatever the reasons, each year many mountaineers of different nations of the world apply for permission to climb Nepal Himalaya, taking up the challenge of formidable hardships. Mountaineering is really called sport tourism. It is being a full-fledged sport, the members applying to climb any of the peaks in Nepal Himalaya, must be physically fit and stout and expert in the use of all needed equipments excellently.

Nepal has fairly established as a good place for adventure and sport tourism. This has amply proved by the increasing influx of international visitors for trekking, white-water rafting, wildlife safari, mountaineering and many other sports. Nepal is well placed to develop certain of these sports and also has the good fortune to attract many devotees and thus benefit from this type of tourism.

Sport tourism refers here the sporting tourism. Of the devotees, which usually causes physical activities and bodily exercises.

Due to the varied features of attractions, Nepal can develop adventure tourism without much emphasis on costly infrastructures. Adventure tourism represents Nepal's actual market potential for the future. Actually, adventure tourism for Nepal is a combination of sightseeing (culture-oriented) and mountaineering and trekking (activity-oriented).

Tourism experts define adventure tourism as the sporting tourism of the devotees of winter sports, nautical sports mountain climbing, horse riding, hunting, fishing, trekking and white-water rafting. Nepal is well placed to develop some of these sports.

Adventure tourism has a big potential for Nepal due to its wilderness and remoteness, apart from the desolate and often forbidding nature. These characteristics have preserved large areas of unique wilderness which provide a potential for recreational demand from the Asian countries, especially the South Asian region, following the increase in standard of living and leisure time is expected to constitute a potential force that will give rise to mountain recreation.

In view of the increase in world tourism and the anticipated trend towards activity-oriented vacation, mountain recreation in the Himalayas could provide an alternative form of vacation.

There are increasing groups of travellers in the developed world which during vacation wish to experience not only sightseeing, moving quickly from place to place or only recreation with inactive beach-hotel life or merely sport (as for instance, trekking) with relatively great bodily exertion and discomforts, but desire, above all, something that is a well-balanced mixture of all these.

Adventure holiday is able to offer everything that an indeterminate group expects of a sporting, recreative and cultural holiday. Moreover, this kind of demand does not correspond to the typical tourist. These tourists, individual travellers from all over the world are already found in small numbers in Nepal. To active demand would be part of a long-term strategy.

Adventure tourism in Nepal supplements and events out the demand for sightseeing and trekking both of which make use of limited parts of the potential offered. On the other hand, it is best for increasing the opportunities of gaining foreign currency and simulating development—both aims of economic policy.

Nepal should concentrate in the long run on the individual tourist category. The risk of mistakes in estimating the existence and size of this tourist group is small since necessary planning of supply for the normal demand will suffice. Nevertheless recreational facilities must be improved and short trekking tours must be developed.

Tourists, wishing to obtain a profound impression of the country during an adventure holiday are more ready to visit places of comparatively less competitive value internationally but which round off the total impression of Nepal, its landscape and people. Such areas are the Terai and the midlands. Wildlife will be of more interest to this group and so in the long term the maintenance and the rehabilitation of national parks and reserve areas will attain greater significance.

In adventure holiday, the tourist should enjoy the real hospitality he expects. This means that all efforts should go to fulfilling his wishes so far as they are necessities. In the sphere of natural things, opening up nature with provision of necessary accommodation for the traveller, and necessary comforts must be suited to the landscape.

Apart from traditional attractions, i.e. mountains, temples, wildlife, there is ample scope for sport activities as an excellent outlet for recreation such as boating, fishing, and white-water rafting. In order to develop adventure tourism, the tourism industry has to tame the landscape for tourists, e.g. short easy paths to viewing sights, camping sites, mountain lodges with adequate comforts in Himalayan valleys at terminal or turning points, supply points, radio links, emergency landing sites where adventure tourist congregate etc.

This opening up of the landscape again must obey the basic rule that it does not destroy the value of what is being opened up.

Adventure tourism represents the most distinctive type of tourism in Nepal and shows a positive trend in demand. Tourism in Nepal is of a highly different and diversified nature. Efforts should be made to popularize adventure tourism among the visitors.

Nepal, no doubt, is an ultimate destination in adventure tourism. It is still the only country which is much of a continent in itself. It displays a unique variety of topography ranging from the tropical places in the south to the arid plateau in the north. The above descriptions give a few of the Himalayan country's adventure areas. And for the independent traveller, there may be more room for new adventures. The wealth is thoroughly pleasant and enjoyable except for the monsoon months.

9

Trekking in the Wilderness

Nepal offers various forms of trekking. It is a vacation paradise. Trekking is really a journey towards the lost horizon. Here is where every day and every mile unfolds new delights and splendours. Here is where the mountain slope combines with a natural wonderland. Trekking provides an opportunity and a thrilling charm by the magnificence of affluence of scintillating natural beauty at every step in the terrain of serene mountain slopes, views lakes, rushing streams and rivers, rolling green countrysides and the warm hearted and hospitable people every where which make relaxation more exhilarating and comfortable.

Trekking in Nepal can provide an opportunity to see and enjoy such wonders as the deepest gorges, snowy peaks, glacier moraines, waterfalls, rocky as well as green hills, national parks and the best of other famous places and sights. No other country offers so many features with a short distance of trekking.

There are many and various types of treks in the mountain areas types of treks in the mountain areas of Nepal. Trekking tours are, therefore, very wide in scope and organized on the basis of the interest of trekkers. There are many licensed trekking agencies which provide a full range of trekking equipments, catering facilities including trekking guides and trekking cooks. Special treks are designed for individuals or groups interested in bird-watching, trekking combined with white water rafting, wildlife safari and observing cultural activities of the common folk. Connoeing in the snow-fed rivers and streams and bathing in the hot springs etc. Trekking is catergorized into two main forms of short and long and it usually covers four regions of the Himalaya, i.e. northern region, central region, eastern Everest region and western region of the country. Before selecting one of the most popular trekking regions, the first trek is also possible by going around the rim of hills of the Kathmandu Valley or around the city of Pokhara. A short trek is designed to give the trekking a brief taste of some major peaks of scenic attractions of particular regions, generally involving four to eight days of walking with the starting point being Lukla for the Everest Region and Pokhara for Annapurna and Gorepani. The first of the most popular trekking regions is around Mount Everest in the east and Pokhara/Annapurna to the west. Longer treks involve more complex itineraries such as to and around the Everest Base Camp, or to Manang, Jomsom. A long trek is usually scheduled for between 23 to 30 days and is organized for more experienced and physically fitter trekking.

A trekking permit is a must for all foreigners to trek in Nepal. Visa extension from the Central Immigration Office, will also be required if the duration of the trek is likely to exceed 30 days. Two passport size photographs are required for permit. Authorized trekking agencies will be able to provide all information, equipment and personnel required for trekking. The trekking season in Nepal commences in September each year and ends in May.

Nepal is famous world-wide for its scenic mountain treks. One of the best ways in which to explore and enjoy the country as a whole is by trekking. It is advisable to make trekking arrangements through a reputable trekking agency which can provide reliable guides and equipment.

Trekkers, as well we know are not homogenenous demand group. A preliminary distinction is formed between group trekker and individual trekkers. They are willingly and moderately equal in number. Group trekkers arrange their trek in advance through international operators who closely affiliate with some local trekking agency. Individual trekkers on the other hand, either use a local trekking agency or make their own arrangements. Some trekkers may use the services of a porter or trek all alone. Variety of trekking tours such as short and long, high and low altitude are available in Nepal. At the same time, 18 peaks of varying heights from 5500 meters to 6630 meters have been declared trekking summits for trekking parties to enjoy adventure in climbing with previous permission from Nepal Mountaineering Association. In Nepal trekking tourism enjoys a distinctly unique market position which is hardly rivalled by any other regional country.

It is but natural that specialised local trekking agencies have developed with the increasing number of trekkers, both organised groups and individuals. This was made active and pioneered by Mountain Travel back in 1963. The connective part of the trekking agencies is represented in the Trekking Agents Association of Nepal which is popularly known as TAAN. This is a national organisation of trekking agencies.

A trekking agency works in anticipation with a specialist operator abroad by arranging all trekking paraphernalia and by actually conducting the trek. These agencies are in a stronger position vis-a-vis their overseas counterparts than are normal travel agencies because of the distinctive quality and uniqueness of Nepali trekking. Trekking can be said without doubt, to build up an independent market. Trekking requires a longer duration of stay and as such there is every possibility to make direct booking for it not making any subsidiary tours to other main attractions. But the figure in 1985 which is minus 33.8% from 1984 calls for vigorous attempts by all trekking agencies to sell and market unique attractions of Nepal directly in the tourist generating markets of the world.

VACATION PARADISE

Trekking in Nepal is a journey to be undertaken on foot for sight seeing in areas where normally modern transport system is not available. Trekking tracks are therefore free of cars, trains, towns and trucks. A hilly region of Nepal are trodden on foot and provide the most enchanting views of Himalayan mountains, green valleys and serene landscapes.

Nepal is rich both in natural scenic beauties and cultural treasures. The only way to get familiar with the people their way of life, their cultural activities and observe from close angle the stupendous natural beauties in trekking. Even a short trekking in any point of Nepal is regarded with sights and scenes of lasting impression.

TREKKING PLACES IN NEPAL

Trekking offers variety and beauty of many sites and scenery; and for the opportunities it offers of becoming acquainted with so many of the different ethnic groups. The trek provides unforgetable scene through magnificent hills, valleys and lakes and the breath-taking views of many Himalayan massifs. Trekking in Nepal can be arranged through trekking agencies. October through May are good months for trekking.

Some Well-Known Treks:

1. Around Kathmandu Valley
   - (a) Dhulikhel (reach by bus or car) to Namoboudha, one day.
   - (b) Bhatkapur to Nagarkot and return via Sankhu: Two days.

2. Kathmandu to Sherpa Villages of Helambu: Seven to eight days around trip.

3. Kathmandu to the Holy Lakes of Gosainkund (not recommended from December to March): Nine to ten days round trip.

4. Kathmandu to Namchebazar: Twelve days. Further to Everest Camp. Additional eight days (Fifteen to twentyfive days around trip with flight from Lukla).

5. Kathmandu to Langtang via Trisuli Bazar. Twelve to fourteen days round trip (once a week flight to Manang also available).

6. Kathmandu to Manang via Dumre (by bus upto Dumre) Fourteen to fifteen days round trip (once a week flight to Manang also available).

7. Pokhara to Gurung Village Chandrung: Four days round trip.

8. Pokhara to Jomsom with flight out of Jomsom: Eight days round trip.

9. Pokhara to Muktinath: Eighteen days round trip.

10. Jumla (reach by air from Kathmandu to Rara Laka: Seven to eight days round trip.

For trekkers with technical climbing expensive, there are moderate Himalayan peaks along the main trekking routes such as Paldor peak (5,894 m) in Langtang region, Tent Peak (5,500 m) in Annapurna region, Lobuje (5,118 m) in Khumbu region.

TREKS AROUND KATHMANDU VALLEY

1. *Shivapuri Trek*: The Kathmandu Valley and its surrounding areas with wide variety of scenery, encompassing views of the majestic Himalaya as well as peaceful rural country side. Shivapuri, north of Kathmandu, is a short trek and provides a panoramic view of the Himalayas from Ganesh Himal in the mid-west to Sagarmatha (Mt. Everest) to the east. This trekking route passes through tiny rural settlements and trekkers can view the daily life of rural Nepal's planting and harvesting of different crops, collecting firewood and fodder or animals etc. This trek is good for bird watching and lovers of plants. Last stop is at Nagarkot. Trekking to the ridge of hill from Shivapuri to Nagarkot is marvellous for viewing different charms of Nepal.

2. *Nagarkot*: This is the name of the hill, 2175 m above sea level. It lies thirty-five kilometers east of Kathmandu. It serves as round-the-year holiday resort. Here is a mini-trek promising a rewarding sunrise view of Mt. Everest and the eastern Himalayan range. From Kathmandu take local transport to Bhadgaon (about half an hour) from the it is a 3 to 4 hour walk to Nagarkot. Accommodation and restaurant are available. Visitors can have closest view of the snow covered Himalayan peaks. Walking up a little to the top of the hill, there is a small pool with the image of Mahadeva known as Mahadev Pokhra. The lofty snow peaks of Gaurishankar, Dorje Lakpa, Chovarvamare and Langtang can be seen. Early morning before sunrise, make the 150 feet climb to the hillcrest far a spectacular view as the morning sun sets one by Manaslu, Cho-Oyu, Lhotse Makalu and Annapurna I, II, III and IV can be seen.

From more ambitious trek, lasting 3 to 4 days, continue from Nagarkot to Shivapuri to Kakani making a hill-top walk around the northern edge of Kathmandu Valley. No trekking permit required but for extension it might be wise to take a sleeping bag and some supplies. It is signed by evergreen pinetrees and the landscape is marvellous. It is necessary to have warm clothing and stout footwear. One can reach to the top of the trekker's route from Kathmandu - Bhadgaon - Kharepati - Gadgade - Nagarkot by car also.

3. *Dhulikhel*: Dhulikhel and the Road to Chinese border. Dhulikhel an ancient town, thirty kilometers east of Kathmandu commands a breath taking view of the Himalayan range. The road to Chinese border links Kathmandu with the Chinese border of Tibet Region. The trekker can enjoy a lot of countryside, panoramic Himalayan view from east to west Himalayan peaks. It has an excellent landscape and serves as the vantage point for viewing the panoramic splendour of the sun rising over the Himalayan summits. It is also a gateway to two famous historic sites of Hindu and Buddhist tradition - Namobuddha and Panauti. Both these places are religious centres and both have retained beauty. It is an easy, exhilarating trek which can cover all places in a single day.

   One could take a taxi or bus or even trek from Kathmandu to Dhulikhel around dawn. On reaching Dhulikhel one should be immediately climb up the hill overlooking the town. From the high point, one can see the sun rising over the glistening peaks of Langtang and in the distant horizon Mt. Everest. It is indeed a fascinating sight and an unforgettable experience. A white stupa emerges against the blue sky. From the stupa, the trail rapidly descends into the Sankhu Valley. The one approaches the outskirts of Panauti.

Panauti is situated at the junction of the Kosi and Panyamatti rivers. It is one of the most ancient and holy places in the Kathmandu Valley. It is a unique site for a Nepali temple architecture. The main cluster of buildings at the ghats consists of a Shiva Temple and a large Dharmasala complete with well preserved, multi-coloured murals. Various other temples with carved wooden struts line the ghats. The way is made up the gentle slope to Dhulikhel.

4. *Birdwatching Treks to Godavari or Nagarjun*: These two places in the Kathmandu valley renowned in arnithological circles. A luxury camp is set up and two or three days are devoted to bird watching in the immediate areas. It is nine kilometers or six miles from Patan city towards the south-east. Here is a fish hatchery. Royal Botanical garden and a marble mine.

5. *Gokarna, Royal Game Sanctuary*: On the banks of the river Bagmati, 8 kilometers (5 miles) lies the lovely Royal Game Sanctuary of Gokaranaban which besides offering hunting, is a charming picnic spot. Many wild animals among them the spotted deer can be seen. On the northern side of Gokarna, on the way to Sundarizal, is the pagoda-style temple of Gokarneshwar Mahadeva overlooking the Bagmati gorges to its right. It is a hillock on which a small village named as Gokarnagaon. Accommodation and elephant ride available in the game sanctuary. This place can be visited by trekking or by car or bus from Kathmandu.

6. *Phulchoki Mountain*: Phulchoki is situated in the east of Kathmandu valley at an elevantion of 2,963 metres (9,720 ft) and one of the prominent peaks surrounding the valley. It is known as the garden of flowers. Here are plenty of flowers such as wide roses, yellow jasmine, iris and other exotica. There is a Buddhist shrine at the top in a midst of a rich grove of rhodo-

dendrons of different colours. This scenic place can be trekked easily in three hours.

7. *Kakani*: Kakani is located between the Kathmandu valley in the south-east and the Trisuli valley in the north-west. It is situated at an elevation of 1,981 meters (6,500 ft.) and a distance of 32 kilometers (20 miles) from Kathmandu. Kakani's features attractions covering from beautiful alpine scenery of the magnificient Himalayan panorama. The snowy ranges of Annapurna, Manaslu, Himalchuli, Ganesh Himal, Chobhamare, Gaurishanker and other can be seen from here in their majestic grandeur. The alluring four peaks of the Ganesh Himal Range are just opposite to it. It commands magnificent views in all sides, snowy mountains in the north and bird's eye view of Kathmandu city in the west. The route passes through the Balaju water Garden and to Kauli—the base of the Kakani mountain. The trekking route is from Kathmandu-Balaju water Garden - Jitpur - Basnet Pauwa - Kakani. There is Tamang settlement. There is a tourists accommodation there. One can reach there by car in about an hour and a half.

8. *Daman*: This place is situated at a distance of 180 kilometers south-west of Kathmandu at an altitude of above 2,400 metres. It is located on the Tribhuwan Highway in between Kathmandu and the border town of Birgunj. There are numerous lookout points along the highway and reveal wide and narrow river valleys, perpendicular ridges, and an ever changing sceneries of nature. It is exhibits some of the loveliest grandeur of Himalayan peaks in all their glory. All Himalayan peaks are seen from here and these are Mt. Everest (8848 m), Dhaulagiri (8,137 m), Annapurna III (7,556 m), Manaslu (8,137 m), Himalchuli (7,892 m), Dorje Lakpa (6,799 m), Langtang (7,246 m), Ganesh Himal (7,406 m), Phurbi Chyachu (6,722 m).

The short sketch of trekking areas in enough to limelight the big potentials of this type of adventure tourism. The following is the short accounts of different areas of Nepal:

— Northern Region, i.e. North of Kathmandu, encompassing mainly Helambu, Gosainkund and the Langtang regions.

— Eastern/Everest Region. This includes not only Everest base camp but also Namche Bazar, Lukla, Thangboche Monastery and the whole Solukhumbu areas.

Other approaches to the Khumbu are possible from the south through Okhaldhunga, Biratnagar, Dharan and Dhankuta. Treks usually last from 21 to 35 days from these routes.

Khumbu can be reached by flying in and out of Lukla. A minimum of 15 or 16 days should be allowed in order to be familiar with this area, including a trip to Base camp or Gokyo lake. Three weeks can easily be spent at altitudes between 3,500 m and 5,500 m.

This region has an enormous attractions such as Mt. Everest, Lhotse, the awesome Ama Dablam, and many other glittering peaks, the famous monasteries of Thyangboche and Thame, the charm of the Sherpa Villages, the beauty of the Gokyo lakes and the stupendous views from Kala Pathar, above Everest Base camp.

Namche Bazar can be reached in 10-14 days trek from Dolalghat Lamosanger or Kirantichaps. A higher, strenuous trail lies to the North through the beautiful Rolwalling Valley, crossing into the Khumbu over the rugged Tashi Lapacha (5,755 m).

— Central region covering all treks whose starting point is Pokhara e.g. Jomsom, Muktinath, Manang and Annapurna sanctuary.

— Western region—mainly Surkhet Jumla and Rara lake.

— Areas open for organised trek through trekking agencies only with the permission of the Ministry of Tourism-Kanchanjunga and Dolpa.

— Trekking agencies also organize treks to less frequented areas such as the far western Nepal and Arun Valley (the world's deepest valley).

— Newly opened trekking areas opened with permission of the Home Ministry - Manasalu and Mustang (Lomanthang).

The newly opened areas include such highly potential places like Olangchungola in Taplejung, Kimatanka in Sankhuwasabha, Lomanthang in Mustang among others.

— Northern Region Helambu, Gosainkund and Langtang.

These trekking areas, directly North of Kathmandu are approached from the Trisuli Valley. These regions are inhabited by Sherpas and Tamangs. Many kinds of different trek can be arranged from 8 to 20 days. Helambu is famous for its natural beauty and wonderful climate. The Gosainkunda lakes lie at over 4,258 m and the pass leading to Helambu 4,610 m is high with the result that this trek spring are ideal and during the monsoon the flora and fauna is exquisite. It is also possible to continue north of Tarkeghyang, the largest of the Sherpa Valleys towards the Ganga La pass.

The most popular trekking routes are listed below for the ever increasing flow the trekkers due to their matchless scenery and unspolled beauty of ancient culture, life style of mountain villagers and tropical jungle to high snowy mountain peaks:

1. *Northern Region*: i.e. to the north of Kathmandu, are Helambu, Gosainkunda, Langtang Valley, and Ganesh Himal etc.

Langtang is a beautiful and remote area with high yak pastures, mixed ethnic groups and one of Nepal's cheese factories. This valley is approached from the Trishuli valley, north of Kathmandu at 3506 m. The return can be made by the same route, or via Gosainkund or the Ganjee La pass and and Helambu. The trek requires 14 to 25 days.

Helambu is famous for its natural beauty and wonderful climate. The snow covered mountains such as Gosainthan, Langtang, Lirung and Jungal Himal can be seen from the route in their superb grandeur. Helambu is about 45 miles north of Kathmandu and covers typical highland Sherpa villages. This region extends from the north of Taramarang to the Gosainkunda Lake and the Lower Jungal Himal foothills. The valley is approached from the Trisuli Valley, north of Kathmandu. The trek usually lasts 8 days.

Gosaikunda is situated at an altitude of 5,100 m. to the north west of Helambu, and 132 kilometers north east of Kathmandu. This is a sacred place of Hindu pilgrimage. The proper trekking route from Kathmandu to Gosainkunda is through Dhunche. While making a trek to Helambu, the return trip can be made by the same route via Gosainkunda, which requires 15 to 20 days. This place is famous for its beautiful landscape, glacial lakes, waterfalls and evergreen forests.

The all weather airport at Biratnagar offers a wide range of treks. Mountain views from the southern area of Everest, Makalu and Kanchanjunga are majestic. To the east of the Arun valley lies the beautiful Milke Danda and Tamur river valley.

Central region: The approach in this region is westwards to Pokhara either by air or highway. The 35 minutes flight from Kathmandu and the journey by road is equally picturesque. The romantic Pokhara valley has three lakes and lies in the interior of Nepal at an elevation of less than 915 m. The m high peaks of the Annapurna range rise almost directly from the plain only twenty five miles away, present a spectacle that is hard to compare any where in the world. Machapuchhare 'fish tail' mountain lies closer and as even more impressive, its huge panorama dominating the valley the variety of treks in this area is endless one can enjoy easy trek passing through orange groves and by lakes with little climbing but excellent view of travel north west to the Kali Gandaki river flowing down from the Tibetan border. There are many trekking areas in this region, i.e. Pokhara to Manang Pokhara to Gurung village of Ghandrung, Pokhara to Jomsom lies in upper Kali Gandaki valley beyond Annapurna and Dhaulagiri Himalayas. It takes about 7 to 8 days to reach there by trekking from Pokhara. It is situated at an altitude of 2713 m. Muktinath is just 18 kilometers North East of Jomsom. There is famous Hindu temple of Muktinath (Lord Shiva) and a Buddhist Gompa surrounded by a series of waterways. It takes almost a fortnight to trek this route. The other region is Manang. Manang is located to the North of the Annapurna range, at an elevation of Annapurna rang 26,545 ft. It can be approached either by way of Muktinath or along the Marsyangdi river of Lamjung. Trekker can also make a circuit trek of Annapurna ranges, Gangapurna Himal, and Kali Gandaki deepest gorge in the world. The trekking route passes through the rhododendron and alpine forests and meadows with highpasses with plenty of landscapes. There is also a fair chance to view the cultural activities of the village folks and their ways of life.

Western Region: The western region has also wonderful places for trekking such as Surkhet, Jumla and Rara lake. Jumla is situated at an elevation of 2,340 m. and it is a forested foothills of pines. Juniper and spruce, the lake Rara is about 28 kilometer far from the main Jumla Bazaar which is connected by air with Kathmandu. This trekking place lies in an isolated and remote part of Nepal. The most enchanting place of wilderness is the Shy Phoksundo National Park. This national park houses blue sheep, Himalayan thar. Himalayan black bear, ghoral, serow, leopard, now leopard and other characteristic species. Thus park is in a trans - Himalayan area in Dolpa district of North western Nepal and the landscape is typically Tibetan with similar vegetations and wildlife. The trek to Dolpa takes 24 days. The maximum altitude of the trek is 5,115 m and this place is reached by taking flight from Kathmandu to Nepalgunj in the southern terai and then to Dolpa by flight from Nepalgunj. Thus region can be reached from Jumla, Dhorpatan and Surkhet. The best time for trekking the region is October, November, March and April. Snowfall in the winter and early spring in this region is very heavy than on the sides of Annapurna and Dhaulagiri areas.

Besides, above described places for trekking, there are areas open for organised trek through trekking agencies only with the permission of the Ministry of Tourism—Kanchanjunga and Dolpa.

Kanchanjunga trek requires 21 days. This is one of the least trekked in regions of Nepal. The trekking route starts from Kathmandu to Mulghat on the plains of the Terai. The trails of eastern Nepal pass on the Tama Kosi, beginning many ethnic groups such as Rai, Limbu, Tamang and Tibetan together. The views of Kanchanjunga, Makalu and Jannu Himals are superb all through the trekking routes.

The route descends to Illam, the final destination for return trip to Kathmandu by bus.

There are other equally famous areas for trekking such as Makalu, the isolated Hongu valley, Gaurishanker, Mera Peak, Hinku valley, around Manaslu, around Dhaulagiri and Jugal Himal etc. Many areas still remain untouched and isolated. Some regions opened recently include Mustang and other 12 northern distracts for trekking. These areas covers more than 50 villages such as upper-Mustang, Dolpo, northern Gorkha, Taplejung and Darchula among others. Mustang is situated north of the main Himalayan chain between snowy mountain on the east and west boardering Tibet. The climate and land is dry and the villages are located in the valley of the altitude of 3,300 m to 4,000 m full of historical sites. It was an important salt trading post in Trans-Himalayan belt. Lo Manthang is surrounded by houses and monasteries enclosed by a wall. Lo-Manthang is the centre of Mustang and it is only walled city in the whole Himalayan region. The people are very poor and their livelihood depend upon the cross-border trade with Tibet.

Trekking is adventurous because all the mountain trails pass through high-rise mountain precipices, ridge-tops and Himalayan riversides providing awe-inspiring moments of the Himalayan beauty and serenely captivating mountain environment. It is often regarded as part of active tourism and can be undertaken by any nature lover. And Nepal has multiple choices of trails ranging from short-distance and less strenuous ones to the long-distance and rigourous trails. Trekking normally ranges from gentle walking around breadth-taking natural surroundings of small hillocks (like the one around the Kathmandu Valley rim and the take district of Pokhara) to the high-altitude trek in the mountains that may take a month or two, depending on the length of the route to trek. Trekking the world's most challenging trails with panoramic scenic grandeur has special fun and glory few trekking enthusiasts would like to miss. Any of the many rigorous trekking trails in mountainous Nepal unfailingly includes unparalleled natural scences of snow-capped mountains, glaciers and cascading Himalayan rivers, strange gorges and to top them all the welcoming hospitality of various ethnic group who are ever cheerful and happy in their lovely costumes.

In comparison to sightseers, trekkers have relatively greater value because of their longer duration in Nepal, ranging from two or three weeks, and their dispersal within the country. They reckon for more of visitor's days as against for sightseers. But the remarkable difference is noticed between organised and individual trekkers in relation to money they spend. Therefore, their economic impact, is distinctively different. Individual trekkers use up less per day and also per tour. The spending, however, happily tend to favour the lower levels of the community. But there is conspicuous capital flowing into the informal sector operators. While looking at the expenditure, trekkers are to be taken in by two categories. The organised trekker, generally, pays out between US $ 15 and US $ 50 per day, relying on the abundant provision of means of ease and pleasure and duration of the tour. The individual trekker who treks alone and accommodates either in his own tent or in an informal lodge, may spend between Rs. 5 and US $ 5. Organised treks, on the other hand, provide jobs and income by employing porters for their trek. As far as the direct marketing of the trekking is concerned, a few local agencies promote the sale of their product directly to their overseas customers. Most allow the marketing to the overseas operator, which indicates that they manage serving the purpose well enough by 30% of the costs involved in trekking packages deal from the United States of America and Europe.

Due to seasonal character and opening of a few attractive trekking areas to trekkers, informal lodges have sprouted along the main trekking routes which make a much more inexpensive trekking possible. The outcome of these development shows that many repeat trekkers are prone to set aside the organised trek for individual trekking. Undercutting has become the order of the day among the trekking agencies themselves. The number of licenced trekking agencies reached to such a high proportion that they are outnumbering the figures of trekkers in analytical and statistical assumption. Naturally, competition among the agencies is vigorous and fearce and causing a condition of a move to individual trekking and produced congestion in all traditional trekking routes.

Trekking tourism is centered in a few areas, so that the possibility of ill-effects that it may bring in, must be looked upon. Trekking tourism has supported really employment and income opportunities, which on behalf of trekking and budget travel are more broadly expanded over a large number of people to-day. It has played an important part in the communities of the flourishing areas where, except it, there is no other economic alternative. Trekking tourism in Nepal can really become perspective and potential if a design or model is cast putting more emphasis to His Majesty's Government's input into planning, development and control.

Trekking is becoming an economic force in the life of the hill and mountain communities and the best potential for generating income and employment. So it is in dire need of regulation and organisation directed at safeguarding the quality and attractiveness of this unique product and the security of those who operate it. The scheme for accomplishing the organisation of existing trekking areas, the determination of perceptible carrying capacities and appropriate monitoring measures, the refinement of trail—side infrastructure the organisation of porters the licencing of properly trained and knowledgeable guides, depots for kerosene or gas, refuse disposal campside planning etc. now need an urgent attention for their prospect of the future. Side by side, the surveyors and feasibility studies are to be carried out to intensify new trekking areas, their capacity, site and suitability to trekking patterns, infrastructures facilities organisation and controls. Proper care and attention are very essential to control over and to sustain the preservation of the cultural and natural environment frequented to trekker's inflow. Top and foremost priority is essential to check uncontrolled trekking activities, keeping eye on the most negative impact they bring along with their development. They now need an organised attempt to improve adverse effects by implementing the measures to suit the carrying capacity on existing routes and opening up of new trekking and to disperse possible development for them in accordance with development objectives of His Majesty's Government of Nepal.

Trekking tourism exhibits the most outstanding type of tourism in Nepal and sets forth a positive trend in demand. Nepal unfolds unique Himalayan attractions with culture personating own element of touristic interest such as the people, their religious shrines, ancient monuments, art treasures and festivals and natural splendous resulting from physical, climatic and ecological features. While these attractions and values set up the essential ingredients for the development of trekking tourism and their economic turn-up is obtained from the economic utilisation of these resources. Tourist attractions can not be transmitted to the market, visitors must come to the site. Accessibility is therefore the most dominant factor. After this, marketing is needed to bring the visitors to the site. Therefore, any tourist attraction taken by itself and not sustained and supported by component elements, may bear little or no economic significance. Scenery and beauty of the natural surrounding embrace an after-image of unmatched variety ranging from the snowy massifs of the Himalayas, lush green valleys abundant of extremely romantic landscape, entering a richly varied wealth of recreational resources. Nepal has got rich and unique setting which features some of earth's most spectacular tourist attractions. So trekking tourism is an enticement not only for adventurer in Nepal, but also stands for an important asset to recreational use and an imploring facet for cultural tourism.

SOLE INDEPENDENT MARKET

Remoteness and inaccessibility have returned large area of unusual wilderness in Nepal which stipulate a potential raw materials for the development of trekking tourism. Unique flora and fauna add an extra indication of the general recreational value. Due to these conditions, trekking tourism is Nepal's only favourable opportunity to build up an independent market. The trekking demands longer duration of stay and for a normal trek makes a visit to other Asian countries quite subsidiary, so that, in any case, direct booking with Nepali tour operators could be made. This fulfills a pre-condition for acquiring foreign currency income besides helping development by diverting the visitors to less developed regions.

The opportunities, provided by recent development are first rate even though, only a fraction of numbers of sightseeing tourists can be achieved. Accurate numbers of current and potential demand are not available. Estimates by available data speak of purpose of visit by trekking and mountaineering equivalent in numbers 15 per cent of all tourists visiting Nepal annually.

The ultimate potentials of trekking tourism in Nepal is vast and varied. These vast potentiality can be materialised only when trekking agencies are eager to provide organised group treks planned long long ahead than relaying on individual treks planned short in advance or spontaneous treks planned in the course of a stay in Nepal. The organised group trek planned long ahead is well prepared and is supplied with full-fledged basic equipments in the best possible way in utmost safety and comfort of the trekkers. The image of Nepal is well represented and this undoubtedly fulfills a pre-condition to develop Nepal's sole independent market for international tourism.

Trekking tourism deserves foreign currency earning but on this respect high import co-efficient must be minimised as much as possible. Development measures must aim at reducing the import co-efficient by fulfilling trecking needs more completely and in a better way by using local products and by building along the trekking routes strong supply points. Another development measure must initiate the local people by means of educational measures, ideas of economic returns and advantages of constructing lodges and inns, cultivating vegetables and fruits, rearing goats, sheep, fish hatching, poultry keeping etc. which the local people will thus get a direct share of the tourist income. This kind of education to the local population might lead to planned way of increasing infrastructures, the necessary prerequisites of cleaning, a fineplace, water and washing place. This will surely infuse a corresponding investment possible. This will also help to curtail all negative effects in the fragile environment.

The trekking agencies, on their part must prepare the detail and practical information by providing good maps supplemented by short description and difficulties, distance and difference in altitude.

Trekking tourism by all means is the singular attraction of Nepal as such as planned development concept of it is to place all efforts now and the future in the extension of this trade and the demand necessary for it to expand. It aims at longer stays in the country which is also a basic condition to attain relative independence in the Asian market and to reach the goals of making this trade as a sole independent market for international tourism.

Trekking is not a wilderness back-packing experience in Nepal but an adventure of scrambling the mountain terrain to explore nature in its most unspoilt beauty wholly free of the unnerving city bustle and mechanical way of life. Trekking in Nepal, no doubt, has now become one of the south-east Asia's booming adventure tourism activities which has caught the sensibilities of all adventure tourists round the world.

10

Rafting in the Snow-fed Rivers

Rafting in the snow-fed rivers is really a captivating travel experience in Nepal. Rafting entangles new thrill in travel where the visitor discovers endless variety of beauty—the ageless enchantments of the picturesque valley, serene and Kaleidoscopic colours and forms of the Himalayas in the horizon the magnetic charms displayed by array of country's avifauna and the flora in line with unspoilt culture and life style of the rural folk. The exciting depth of the deepest gorge in the world cleave by tectonic snow-fed rivers flowing through the continual binding in turbulent flow, all create marvel of excitement and wonder. To the avid adventurer, rafting in the turbulent rivers of Nepal, produces nerve thrilling incident of strange and wonder stricken astonishment.

The pleasure of rafting on the cascading water of Nepal offers an unforgettable experience. Rafting is all season sports and just one of many unique adventure exclusive to Nepal. Rafting in the rivers of Nepal during winter is a suitable time which creates the most interesting and varied pattern in the world—taking from the thickly forested valleys through rock, gorges into open sub-tropical plains—all in a few days. The sensation of the rafting moving through terrain, wildlife and river side villages is dramatic and a best for the photography and visual attraction.

Nepal's steep land relief and high-rise mountains and gigantic hills crisscrossed by numerous juvenile rivers emanating from the Himalaya have all made adventure rafting the number one water sport. The fun and adventurous feeling inherent in any rafting trip in Nepal pulls a crowd of rafting enthusiasts during the season. Rafting is practically a seasonal engagement, for the rainy season is not a proper time for rafting on Nepal rivers. The pleasure of white water rafting on the torrentially gushing waters of the Trisuli Sunkoshi, Kaligandaki and Arun rivers offers an unforgettable experience. As the Himalayan rivers are full of rapids of varying intensity, a rafter of any degree of daring and rafting calibre finds the Nepal rivers ideal for both pleasure and adventure.

Normally, professional rafting trips operated by numerous rafting agencies in the country range from one day to several weeks, depending on the length of the river and the preference of the rafters. Rafting trips can either be a smooth scenic float down a calm, shallow river or more adventurous one on wild river. Sight-seeing in Nepal on a rafting is another marvellous experience. Rafting in the snow-fed rivers was introduced in 1974 in Nepal and its popularity has been growing day by day ever since.

River rafting in the tectonic snow-fed rivers of Nepal offers exciting journey for adventure, an exceptional opportunity to experience ecstasy of uncredible real that is destination Nepal. The pleasure of rafting on the blistering water of Nepal's rivers offers memorable experience. Rafting in the major rivers of Nepal has becoming popular with adventurous rafters as it is one more means of familiar with countryside and ethnic life-style while enjoying the thrill of adventure. The three most commonly rafted rivers now are the Sun Koshi, the Trisuli and the Seti and there are also other more exciting and challenging rivers.

Eight rivers in the three river systems are open for rafters for river rafting. The popular rivers are the Trisuli, the Kaligandaki, the Bheri, the Seti, the Sunkoshi, Karnali, Tama Koshi and the Arun. For the purpose of river rafting, the following rivers are in use:

1. Sapta Koshi River System (East Nepal).
2. Narayani or Sapta Gandakai River System (Central Nepal).
3. Karnali River System (West Nepal).

To be more elaborate about the river systems of Nepal, the precise information is given for clarify:

> *East Nepal*: The Sapta Koshi — the feeders are Indravati, Sun Koshi, Tama Koshi, Likhu Khola, Dudh Koshi, Arun and Tamor.
>
> *Centre Nepal*: The Krishna—Kali Gandaki on the north and Narayani on the south. The feeders are Trisuli, Budhi Gandaki, Daraundi, Seti, Madi, Kali and Andhi.
>
> *West Nepal*: Karnali with feeders Seti and Bheri.

As mentioned above Nepal's river courses generally parted into three systems in accordance with their origins. The first division consists of the three main river system of the country—the Koshi, Gandaki and Karnali river systems, all of them having their sources from glaciers and snow-fed lakes. The Koshi river system eventuates of the Tamor, Arun, Dudh Koshi, Likhu, Tama Koshi, Sun Koshi and Indravati rivers. The sources of Arun and Sun Koshi lie on Tibet. The confluence of these rivers is at Tibeni (near Dharan) in Sagarmatha zone. Flowing for almost 10 kilometers through a narrow gorge before reaching the plains, the "Sapta Koshi" or Koshi expanded with the waters of the seven rivers, ultmately plunge into the Ganges in India.

The Gandaki river system in Central Nepal is composed of the Kaligandaki, Budhigandaki, Marsyngdhi, Trisuli, Seti Madi and Darundi rivers. The Kaligandaki is the longest river and the Trisuli, the main tributary of this system. The Kaligandaki originates in Mustang and mingles with the Trisuli at Deoghat in Chitwan. The river is then called Narayani and flows to join in India.

The Karnali river system in Western Nepal consists of the Humla Karnali, Mugu Karnali, Seti and Bheri rivers and is considered to be the longest river system in the country. The Humla Karnali, which has its source in Tibet, is the main tributary. This river assumes the name Gogra after entering India.

There are rivers of second category like the Mechi, Mahakali, Bagmati, Kamala, Rapti etc., which have their sources in the Mahabharat range. The Bhagmati river is the principal river of the Kathmandu Valley which has its source at Baghdwar and flows out through the Chobar Gorge. There are many other streams and rivulets having their origins from the Chure Hill constitute the third category coming out of monsoon rains and otherwise dry.

River rafting has become another type of adventure tourism in Nepal. Many rafting agencies organise "Combination trips" consisting of trekking and rafting or alternatively a raft down the Trisuli river to Royal Chitwan National Park followed by two or three day stay at one of the Park's hotels or lodges. Rafters can arrange rafting trips at Trishuli, Sun Koshi, Arun Tamor and Seti rivers and enjoy jungle excursions at National Parks. The reality of Himalayan rivers are more than rafting, it is physically exciting, culturally interesting and visually appealing.

Nepal's major rivers like the Narayani, the Karnali and the Sapta Koshi can provide wonderful river raft experience. Rafting trips are of varying duration and as described above take place on such rivers as the Trisuli, Narayani, Marsyangdhi, Seti and Sun Koshi. Many kinds of river rafting from one day to as many as fifteen days duration are organised. Combined river rafting trips can be arranged with trek and this kind of trips vary from 11 to 18 days. The kind of adventure package provides singular and magnificent vacation that can not be experienced in any other part of the world. The friendly and welcoming villages on the way provide another attraction to river rafting. River rafting usually gives rafters a unique insight into village life. It also provides glimpses of wildlife such as wild buffaloes, deers, the fresh water dolphins, crocodiles etc, occasionally per chance, leopards and tigers might be seen on the river bank.

There are popular water-ways for river rafting. There are many possible routes for river rafting. Among them, some of the popular water ways for rafting are: Gajuri to Kuringhat (two days), Muglin to Narayanghat (two days), Muglin to Tiger Tops, Chitwan (three days), Charaundi to Tiger Tops, Chitwan (four days), Damauli to Tiger Tops, Chitwan (three days), Dolalghat to Chatttara (eight days) and so on.

Given below are the names of the rivers and sectors for information:

River	*Sector*
1. Arun	Tumlingtar—Chatara
2. Bheri	Birendranagar—Chisapani
3. Karnali	Bhankhet—Chisapani
4. Kaligandaki	Krishna—Royal Chitwan National Park, Chitwan
5. Seti	Damauli—Royal Chitwan National Park, Chitwan

6. Sun Koshi	Dolaghat to Chatara
7. Tama Koshi	Basti—Chatara
8. Trisuli	Trisuli—Narayanghat.

One can discover unique adventure by rafting in Nepal. Rafters explore many exhilarating experiences in always shifting currents and foam-laced whirlpool in the rivers of Nepal. River rafting offers the rafters cities of art treasures, beautiful resorts, picturesque lakes, colourful banks, majestic snow-capped Himalayas, resplendent valleys, seasonal festivals, cultural events and a gay social life. At the sametime, river rafting provides magnificent views here is where rafters will find vacation fun and beauty. Here is where everyday, every kilometer infolds new delight and thrills. The trip allows the rafters to experience in some of the high current rivers like Seti. Marsyangdhi for one or two days executing a beautiful scenery to the beautiful landscapes extending from the mountain views to the endless Terai plains of the Southern parts of Nepal. The rivers said to be the world's best for rafting experience flow through evergreen forest with seldom views of the snowy mountain peaks. It also gives an opportunity to see the colourful community living by the river bank.

There are choice and variety of river rafting in Nepal. River rafting trips can be organised from 1-22 days. All major water ways of Nepal are used for river rafting. Most popular trips are on more remote rivers accessible only on foot. A trek with river rafting is an opportunity to continue two distinctly different ways of seeing Nepal. Combined trips such as the Sun Koshi Raft Expedition and remote wildlife viewing last from 12 to 10 days. One day raft trips are usually on the Trisuli river. Trisuli river has exciting rapids and scene stretches. Individually designed raft excursion for any length of time or dry river can be arranged. Licenced rafting agencies provide inflable rubber rafts with a seating capacity of up to six persons including the agency guide. Rafting trips down the calm shallow rivers or more adventurous "white water" rafting where one has to shoot the rapids. Licenced rafting agencies arrange rafting comfortably. Cost includes per person per day inclusive of all land transportation accommodating in inflated rubber rafts serviced by experienced rafters and guides, all meals, sightseeing and exploration, life jackets and fully equipped over night camping. Most enterprising rafting trip begins from Damouli to Narayanghat. Damouli is located approximately 160 km west of Kathmandu to Pokhara. This river is the tributary of the Sapta Gandaki river. Saranghat Village on hill touches this water ways where the river joins with Trisuli river and the landscape begins to change from middle hill to Terai plains with sandstone and gravel. Devighat, the Hindu pilgrimage spot on Narayani river bank comes on the way.

Attributing to the instability and variableness on Nepali's rivers, seceding as much as thirty/forty times in height between the dry season and the monsoon period, transportation by water courses is not commonly used. Log floating is a regular phenomenon in the upper Gandaki river and small boats have been used on the upper Koshi river. Possibilities for pleasure boating in the rivers of Nepal are ample if only the rivers are made easier to reach and thus utilizing them as means of transport in the future as a tourist attraction.

The development of rafting is gaining much more importance at present that it is rapidly becoming substantial tourist industry. It is also becoming major motivation for many incoming international visitors to Nepal. International visitors are now considering themselves that their holidays can be much more pleasant if they can arrange rafting as a part of their Nepal vacation. Rafting in the rivers of Nepal being a most important human and economic factor is also considered a vital tourist activity in Nepal.

Nepal presents a broad variety of river rafting. All the major rivers of Nepal are used for rafting. This sport is scientifically and commercially established at present. It has become popular adventure trip in Nepal. The rivers of Nepal are attracting many international rafters because of the large number of wild and untrained waves in them. The rivers provide difficult obstacles and no two rivers are the same. The rivers are flowing through wilderness areas and floating over a steep river Canyon, valley of lush forest land in the plains of southern Nepal. Rafting in Nepal, in general, goes through series of wanderings which provide wildlife viewing in their natural habitat at close angle. River rafting provides a panorama—unusual such as gueshing with whizzing sound flushing and dovetailing in strong foaming currents. Such experience is obtained in West Nepal adventure in West Nepal Karnali river rafting. This river carries rafters from put-in-point to Royal Bandia National Park. This park is at the foot of the Siwalik hills where the Karnali ceases its violent descent and flows smoothly out of the Karnali gorge at Chisapani. The Karnali river is dotted with reverent forested islands which afford natural protection for the wildlife. The tented camp situated on banks of the Karnali river designed after famous Tiger Tops tented capms at Royal Chitwan National Park. Rafting here goes through series of wanderings which provide wildlife viewing—tiger leopard, wild elephant, black buck, swamp deer, chital sambhar, blue bull, wild boar, sloth bear, serow, ghoral as well as marsh mugger and the endangered gharial crocodiles in their natural habitat at close angle.

Since Himalayan River Excursion as indicated before introduced white water Rafting in Nepal as organised way with a paid trips in 1997. This river rafting business is annually increasing. Rafting provides direct and indirect employment to about 1500 Nepali and contribute some about 1,50,000 to 700,000 Rupees to the national treasury.

As exemplified above eight of the Nepal's snow-fed rivers are open for rafting purpose so far. Rafting as an adventure sport is gaining popularity every year. Rivers like the Trisuli and Sun Koshi are becoming most popular and sought after rafting rivers by foreigners in Nepal. By recent analysis 65% of the rafters like the Trisuli river for rafting. Both the rivers Trisuli and Sun Koshi are near to the Kathmandu and easily accessible and so they are most popular. It is reviewed that Five to seven per cent of international tourists go rafting on the Sun Koshi, Trisuli, Seti, Gandaki, Kali Gandaki, Bheri and Karnali rivers. Rafting in such a way has distinct potentials for attracting visitors and providing employment. There is a tremendous potential for rafting adventure. It is officially recorded that 5114 visitors enjoyed rafting in 1993 and His Majesty's Government of Nepal collected Rs. 40,91,20 in 1993. There are more than 77 registered rafting agencies at present.

tribute for a third to the Himalayan mountain system. Between the Kanchenjunga massif to the Mahakali river lie more than thirteen hundred peaks with an altitude of more than six thousand metres. These peaks can be set apart as follows:

> About eight thousand metres—eight of the fourteen highest peaks in the world.
>
> About seven thousand metres—one hundred and twenty seven peaks.
>
> About six thousand metres—one thousand and one hundred sixty six peaks.

Nepal Himalayas consist of many outstandingly beautiful mountain groups. The Kanchenjunga Himal forms the eastern most precinct of the Nepal Himalaya casting a wall of cragged peaks. The Kanchenjunga range constitutes the border point between Nepal and Sikkim. One of the most impressive of the Himalayan giants, it is the third highest peak in the world having 8586 metres (main summit). The name Kanchenjunga signifies "five treasures of great snow", and it is a peak with four lumps to all the four cardinal parts. The eastern part as entirely in Sikkim but it sends down Yaling, Yamatane, Janndu, Lamtang and Kanchenjunga glaciers to Nepal. The main summit of this mountain had been attempted since 1905 and was first climbed half a century later.

Khumbu Himal is another group of Nepal Himalaya which has the greatest concentration of peaks. It has many 6,000 meter peaks and four above 8000 meter peaks dominated by Sagarmatha (Mt. Everest—8848 m), the highest peak in the world. While the main range forms a bend along the Sino-Nepal border the many extended spurs beset glaciated valleys of Barun, Imja, Khumbu, Dudh Kosi and Nengpo Dzangpo.

The high ranges of Kanchenjunga system and Khumbu Himal are spaced out by the great gorge to the Arun and the 6000 meter peaks. The Khumbu Himal with extensive glaciers and the compressive peaks rising to the north, west and east around the upper belts of the Dudh Kosi river is one of the most interesting mountaineering centres in Nepal.

Khumbu Valley is the home of world famous Sherpas and is undoubtedly one of the most impressive places due to the grandeur of its vast glaciers, lofty peaks, magnificent pastures, meadows and the mountain villages. Sherpas are known world over for their climbing experiences. Some of the important villages of the region are Namche Bazar (3,440 m), Khumjung (3,790 m), Thami (3,800 m) Phortse (3,849 m), Tengboche (3,867 m) and Pangboche (3,985 m). Much of the area in Khumbu Himal has been included within the Sagarmatha National Park.

Some of the prominent peaks with Khumbu Himal are Sagarmatha (Mt. Everest, 8848 m), Lhotse (8,516 m) Lhotse Shar (8,400 m), Cho Oyu (8,201 m), Chachung Kang I (7,952 m), Nuptse I (7,855 m), Pumo Ri (7,161 m), Numbur (6,957 m) and Ama Dablam (6,812 m). Ama Dablam is regarded as the most awesome peak in the Khumbu Himal Group.

The name Sagarmatha in Nepal means 'the head of the sky or the peak Kissing Clouds'. This region is itself a glittering marvel of spectacles of many snowy mountains, glaciers, alpine flowers, natural vistas and man-made monasteries. The first maiden expedition was made in 1921 by Lt. Col. C. K. Howard Bury. After this, many expeditions were carried on Sagarmatha. Finally British expedition led by Col. John Hunt successfully put two team members, Edmund Hillary and Tenzing Norgay on the peak on May 29, 1953. Lured by the challenges of the highest peak in the world, climbing teams from different nations apply for expedition annually.

Kumbhakarna Himal, another Nepal Himalayan group, is situated west of the Khumbu Himal to the upper sides of Arun river. This is dominated by Makalu (8,463 m) the fifth highest peak in the world. The Arun River Valley is a picturesque spot in beautiful setting. It is rich in various climate and vegetation levels right up to the glacial wilderness. This group is also popular for mountaineering expeditions.

Rolwaling Himal lies east of Tamba Kosi and is composed of two parallel ranges on either sides of Rolwaling Chu. The northern range strikes west of Menbing La and forms the boundary between Nepal and People's Republic of China. The prominent peaks of this group is Gauri Shankar (7,134 m) named after Hindu God Shankar and his Consort Parvati and Choba Bhamare (6,116 m). This peak of Choba Bhamare stands a loof west of the Rolwaling Himal group and east of Kodari.

Gauri Shankar peak is majestic due to its changing shape Rolwaling was once a glacial valley and a visit to this place gives the impression of walking in the surrounding of the mountains. Melungtese (7,181 m) and Chobutse (6,700 m) and Dorje Lakpa (6,966 m), Jugal and Lamgtang Himal with their snow peaks dominate the landscape north of Kathmandu. They form a 20 kilometer long sharp ridge between Nayanam Phy glacier (Tibet) and Lamgtang glacier (Nepal). Jugal Himal is the nearest Himalayan range from Kathmandu.

Extending from the Jugal Himal in the east to the Rasua Garhi Pass in the west and circumscribed by the Trisuli river in the west and Lamgtang Khola in the south are the commanding fence of the Lamgtang Himal permeated by Langtang Lirung (7,234 m), the tallest peak in this group. There are various peaks east of the Langtang Lirung as extension of Shisha Pagmas in Tibet. There are two resorts of Helambu and Gosainkund at the southern side of the Langtang group. The Langtang Valley offers grand views of the Himalaya, wood-lands, meadows and beautiful villages. Langtang Lirung was firstly climbed by the Japanese team of mountaineers in 1959.

Ganesh and Kutang group lie between Bhote (Trisuli) Kosi and Trisuli river. Ganesh Himal soars abruptly west of Chilime Khola with Palder (5,896 m) as its auxiliary peak. The western Kutang Himal defines the boundary between Nepal and People's Republic of China. This region is luxuriant in vegetation, superb views, splendid villages and welcoming people. Ganesh Himal in all its magnificence is also visible from Kathmandu Valley. Ganesh Himal group has five peaks i.e. Ganesh I, II, III, IV and V peaks. Ganesh Himal I was successfully conquered by Franco-Swiss in 1955.

Gorkha Himal stands from the Budi Gandaki river in the east and the Marshyangdi river in the west. The principal peaks in the Gorkha Himal group are Baudha (6,672 m), Peak 29 (7,871 m), Himalchuli (7,893 m) Manaslu (8,163 m) etc.

Gorkha Himal group is seen in all its prominence from several points along the Marshyangdi, the Budi Gandaki river valleys, Lamtang and the valley of Kathmandu.

On the southern side lies the high mountain of lower Himalayas known as Barach Pokhari Lekh which gives the most beautiful view of the range.

Annapurna and Damodar compose one of the most impressive ranges in central Nepal. Annapurna Himal stretches between the Marshyagdi and Kali Gandaki rivers. It has a long northern spur west of Manang but is linked with Damodar Himal and the border range east of Mustang. The main Annapurna range can be seen as prominent attraction from Pokhara Valley as well as Manang Valley. A narrow ridge south of Annapurna III (7,555 m) is crowned by the impressive peak of Machhapuchhre (6,997 m) between the Seti and Madi Valleys.

Damodar Himal has numerous modest peaks. It joins Lugela Himal at Brikuti Shail (6,334 m) and turns north.

Annapurna has four peaks having the height of 8091 m, 7,939, 7,555 m and 7,525 m respectively. Another peak, Gangapurna is 7,455 metres in height. Annapurna I was climbed successfully by French in 1950.

Dhaulagiri, a massive ridge with high peaks, stands between the Kali Gandaki river and Bheri river. The main ridge has an east-west course and long spur slopes north to Mukut Himal and then reaches further to the border ranges in Muktinath. Dhaulagiri-I (8,167 m) has five high peaks and all of them are very impressive. Another peak, Churen Himal, is 7,371 metre high.

Dhaulagiri is one of the most majestic peaks in the Himalayan range. It is the embattled rampart of many mountaineering expeditions. This peak was firstly climbed by a Swiss team in 1960.

The Kanjiroba Dolpa and Humla group of Nepal Himalaya which culminates in Kanjiroba peak (6,883 m) along with another 28 peaks exceeding 6,000 metres extends between Bheri river and Humla Karnali. This group does not form large impressive range but rather an extensive bewilderment of spurs and peaks of intermediate height. Phoksundo TSO lake, one of the most beautiful lakes of Nepal, lies to the south west of the Kanjiroba Himal. The beautiful valley of Mugu provides magnificent views of snowy ranges. Tribrikot is the main village which is located at the southern side of the Kanjiroba Himal.

Saipal and Byas Pushi Himal group of Nepal Himalaya covers the area west of Humla Karnali mountains. Saipal settles as an isolated group of snow peaks. The highest peak rises to 7,831 metres ringed by many subsidiary peaks.

The Byas Rishi Himal forms the western limit of the Nepal Himalaya. These two important groups are separated by the upper valleys of the Seti river. The western group is known as the Byas Rishi Himal and the eastern as the Saipal Himal. The principal peaks are Api (7,132 m), Nampa (6,775 m) in Byas Rishi Himal group and Saipal (7,031 m) in Saipal group.

The whole area of the southern part of the Api-Nampa—Saipal group provides ample opportunities for magnificent mountaineering activities. It is popular for the great scope, it provides to the mountaineers.

The Nepal Himalayas, the majestic splendour enclosing earth's "Third Pole", have embraced the greatest concentration of high peaks, so many still to be climbed and glaciers to be explored. Due to these reasons, the Nepal Himalayas are much popular among the mountaineers of the world. So mountaineering in Nepal started from mid-twentieth century and the remarkable chapter of mountaineering started from 1949/1960. After this, extensive mountain climbing activities paved the way for expeditions up to the present. The Nepal Himalayas having the height of 6,000 metres to 8848 meters are annually climbed. The number of mountaineering teams from different nations is increasing annually and popular peaks are looked far ahead. It is the lure of the glittering peaks and project of conquests which attract all o them to scale the highest mountains in the world. The Himalayas of Nepal, marvellous creation of nature and priceless heritage of the world, have now become the top most mountaineering attractions.

The Great Himalayas of Nepal and their peaks are covered up with snows throughout the year. They are awe-inspiring blend of snow-capped peaks, towering cliffs, heavy glaciers, gaping ravines and deep gorges. They are the loftiest mountain ranges in the world and includes the world's highest and also the most lovely peaks. They are of exceptional interest for the mountaineers and are undoubtedly attractive scenic spots in the world.

Ever since the country was first opened to climbers in 1949, the Himalayas of Nepal have become a centre of mountaineering activities. There have been about 570 small and large expeditions to explore and climb peaks during the period 1949—1980 and their impression of success and failure have given impetus to more men to scale and to explore unknown mysteries of the Nepal Himalayas. From 1980 to the present, there were too many expeditions to list in detail. During the 1990 alone as many as 120 expeditions attempted to scale different peaks of the Nepal Himalayas.

Latest figures of mountaineering 1997 are recorded as total number of team 49, total number of mountaineers 375, successful team 24, number of persons employed 3,813, casualty to foreigners 4, casualty of Nepali 3 and His Majestys's Government of Nepal earned Rs. (in 100) 67287.

Each year, the mountaineers from all over the world in all seasons take up the challenge of the Nepal Himalayas. The number of mountaineering team is increasing annually and popular peaks are booked for climbing years ahead. It is the lure of the unknown and the prospect of conquests and adventures which attract the climbers of all the countries. The Himalayas of Nepal, a unique creation of Nature and priceless heritage of the world have now become the top in mountaineering activities. Nepal Himalayas are now climber's nightmare.

The Nepal Himalayas have been the centre of attraction to the whole world through all ages as a place of pilgrimage or penance to a saint, calm and quite natural grove for philosopher to dip in his search, vast field of search for researcher and mountaineer. The icy pyramid of Nepal Himalayan peaks are the enchanting examples of the serenity and they overwhelm sights. They are the splendour of unspoiled beauty and they cast a panorama which is as vast as they are fascinating and scintillating spills which have put a symbol of calmness and serenity and a mystical charm to land. All these peaks have been the single-most dream of all mountain expedition heroes round the world. The legendary triumphs of the heroes of mountaineering have made the country so popular in the world that the aspiration of conquering them, the mighty peaks has invoked immense desire among seasoned mountaineers to try an assault on the Himalaya. The number of mountaineering teams hoping to win over the high Himalayan peaks has been constantly on the increase over the last ten years. The growth of adventure tourism in Nepal was virtually impossible without the Himalayas. Referring to the growth of adventure tourism in Nepal, Sir Edmund Hillary, mountaineering hero and pioneer Everest conqueror, said that with mighty mountains, great rivers, ancient culture and friendly people—"Nepal is one of the world's fastest growing adventure tourism areas". Mountaineering and trekking are of considerable importance for Nepal, because normally mountaineers and trekkers stay here for a longer period of time than other sight-seers. Nepal is obviously a global centre of mountaineering.

12

Wildlife Tourism

Nepal has a rich and varied species of flora and fauna. These comprise an important part of Nepal's national culture and heritage. They also furnish scientific, educational and re-creational value to mankind. The creation of the National Parks and Reserves are therefore very necessary to ensure their conservation.

There was no mechanism for conservation of wildlife in the past and no thought was given for to protect living heritage. The Terai Jungle in the south, bordering India were widely famed for their wildlife. Big game shootings were organised and many tigers and rhinoceroes were killed. It was here in the year 1876 that Maharaja Jung Bahadur Rana arranged a big shoot for King Edward VII (then Prince of Wales). Again in 1890, Maharaja Bir Shumsher Rana invited Prince Albert Victor to a shoot in the terrain Naya Muluk Terai. In such a way, great organised hunts were held in different times and periods and many tigers, rhinocerous as well as hundred of deers, pigs and others species were killed. But such great organised hunts were normally held at interval of several years. While speaking about the abundant and varied fauna, Mr. E. A. Smythies, B. A. (Oxon), C.I.E in his book BIG GAME SHOOTING IN NEPAL, 1942 in the following way: "It is scarcely surprising that the Terai has always been regarded as a sportsman's paradise.

When King George V came in 1911 to shoot in the Nepal Terai and again when the Prince of Wales came ten years later, wonderful collections of live animals of Nepal were presented by the Maharaja to His Majesty and H.R.H., to enrich the zoological gardens of the Empire". So Nepal was very rich in the field of wonderful avifauna of different species.

Even after big game shooting after many years interval, there were ample abundance of wildlife to fill the stocks due to virgin forest of Nepal supplying lands and foods. It is better here to have some idea about the physiography of Nepal, keeping vision to the climatic factor and altitude. The country can be divided into three regions as follows:

— The southern lowland which covers the plains, Terai and Churia (Siwalik) foothills up to 1,525 m.

— The central region which includes the Mahabharat and central hill ranges and valleys from 2,000 m to 3,050 m.

— The alpine zone which comprises the main Himalayan chain and peaks above 2,750 m to 8,840 m.

These three regions have a fauna and flora which are characteristic of these distinct specialities. The lower Terai region is covered by thick tropical forest. The tree species constitute Shorea robusta with many other species such as Schima wallichii, Jamun, Kadam, Kusum, Simal, Siris, Sissau etc. Along with valuable trees, there are savannahs of thick and long grasses, having twice the size of an elephant. The Churia hills are rich in tall Pinus longifolia. Many kinds of orchids are seen blooming at their different colours and attractions. Then the central region as well as Alpine zone have different variety of willows, evergreen oaks, rhododendrons, conifers side by side with berch, alder, hornbeam, elm poplar and walnut. But dwarf rhododendron, Juniper and birch are noticed in the high Himalaya. Alpine vegetation is covered with a vigours growth of grasses, herbs and shrubs. Going higher in the Himalayan zone, the plants cover becomes more and more thin and sparse until the alpine barrren rock and perpetual ice and snow. Caragana shrubs also occur in the alpine zone. Grey moss trailed on the branches and virginia creepers draped their flowers on the tree trunks. Gentians and red berries are also noticed along with cluster of gentians on the cliffs.

The Terai has more varied fauna. The immense forests are the abode of the Royal Bengal Tiger, and leopard, the sloth bear, the wild elephant, the one-horned rhinoceros and the wild buffalo. There are deer species such as sambhar, swamp deer, chital, parpha, mouse deer etc. The antelopes as the black buck, four-horned antelope and wild pig. Smaller animals as the fishing cat, leopard cat, common jungle cat, small civet, squirrels, the pangilon are also available. Regarding birds the peacock, jungle fowl, black partridge and migratory duck and geese are also noticed in the Terai.

The central region has also a abudant fauna. The leopard, clouded leopard, tiger civet, Himalayan civet and paradoxurus. Jackals, wilddog, fox, the black Himalayan bear, badger are noticed along with flying squirrels, the serow, gural, the musk deer and the red barking deer.

In the high alpine zone, species and animals are comparatively few and include the leopard and marmot, bharal, ibex and tahr representing the sheep and goats, yak and the rare Tibetan stag. The bird species are blood pheasant, the handsome tragopan and the beautiful Monal. There are also bird species represent Lammergeyer, snow cock, snow partridge, clough and buntage, red starts and dippers. A birds ibis bulls are also seen on migration from Tibet. In such a way, wild extremities of nature have their own wildlife on high alpine zone, cuddly little creature called mouse hares are also seen scurried among the boulders of the glaciers moraine. Blue sheep with enormous curved horns are in Dolpa and Humla in rocky section with large curving horns and thick grey mantle. There is yeti or Abominable snowman, a strange creature that the local people consider its home among the mountains.

Nepal is very rich in wildlife heritage conservation of nature in the past has been entrusted to the Forest Department of His Majesty s Government and it has been not able to manage properly due to lack of funds and trained staff. But distinction of habitat and environment was increased at an alarming way and some noval ideas were taken to save the determinating natural loss due to population growth and urbanisation. The loss incured in the past realised at present and wildlife protection is thought to carry on in proper management and planning.

Nepal has been started a National Park and wildlife section in 1971 but conservation began only in 1973 in collaboration with FAO/UNDP. Ecological surveys have been carried out and ways and means are found out for suitability for Preserves or National Parks. After this, His Majesty's Government of Nepal initiated a National Park and Wildlife Conservation Project. The first area to become a National Park was Chitwan. Royal Chitwan National Park was first gazetted National Park in 1973, enlarged to the present size in 1977 protects the last surviving population of Great one-horned rhinos as well as other endangered species as the Royal Bengal Tiger, Bison, Gangetic dolphin and Gharial Crocodiles. This is situated in the inner Terai southwest of Kathmandu. The area of the park is 932 sq. kms and has been included in the World Heritage List in 1984 by the World Heritage Committee. This is one of Nepal's largest forest region with a wide range of wildlife.

After the establishment of Royal Chitwan National Park, the next landmark in wildlife conservation was the opening of Sagarmatha National Park in 1976. Due to a large number of trekkers to the Mount Everest Region, deforestation had become a major problem in the area causing in the alarming threat in wildlife. So this park is established in 1976 to supervise development towards preserving environment and the indegenous wildlife to thrive. This Park covers the Everest Region of north-eastern Nepal and is the home to the Sherpa people as well as high altitude mammals as musk deer, Himalayan Tahr, serow, leopard, black bears, Himalayan wolf, marmot and Nepal's National bird Danfe (Lophoporus) and pica. This park is 1148 sq. kms and lying above 3,500 m. altitude. This park is also encluded in the World Heritage List. Vegetations consist of rhododendrons, birch, blue pine, juniper and silver fir. Then, six National Parks, three Wildlife reserves, two Conservation Areas and one Hunting Reserve have established now in order to maintaining and developing ideal wildlife habitats. Royal Bardia National Park is situated in the southwest Terai of Nepal along the Karnali and Babai rivers. This park is upgraded from a Wildlife Reserve in 1988. This park is famous for Gharial Crocodiles and Gangetic dolphin. It is a habitat for tiger, spotted deer, black buck, sambhar deer, wild boar and swamp deer plus more than 350 species of birds. It is spread over 968 sq. kms.

Langtang National Park is Nepal's second largest protected area. It is 1710 sq. kms. and lies along the main Himalayan range. This park has a varied ecology from subtropical to mountain alpine. This park harbours wild bear, Himalayan Black Bear, ghoral, leopard, grey langur monkey. The musk deer and Himalayan tahr are found in the alpine and sub-alpine regions. Birds like Impeyan, blood Monal and Kaliz pheasant are commonly seen as well as chuckor and grey partridge. Red Panda is one of the park's rearest wildlife species.

Shey-Phoksundo National Park is of 3555 sq. kms and covers the rich forest of the lower Himalayas and near desert like terrains of the Trans-Himalayan region and Tibetan types of flora and fauna. This park established in 1984. Its exact location is in the Karnali zone in Dolpa. The vegetations are pure walnuts, willow, oak, poplar and cypress. The wildlife includes blue sheep, goral, musk deer, leopard, wild dog, marmot, weasel, mouse hare, rhesus and common monkeys.

Rara National Park is a small mountain Park of 106 sq. kms, north of Jumla in western Nepal situated in the back of the Rara Lake, the largest lake at an elevation of 3000 meters. This park is the home of black bear, red Panda, yellow throated marten, goral, serow, Himalayan tahr and musk deer. Birdlife comprises of Impeyan blood Monal and Kaliz pheasants. This park is full of magnificent conifer forests.

Khaptad National Park lies in far western Nepal. Established in 1985, it covers 225 sq. kms. This park is a rolling plateau of grass land and forests which habitat leopard, Himalayan black bear, wild dog, wild boar, musk deer, ghoral, Himalayan tahr and many species of birds.

Makalu-Barin National Park covers 2330 sq. kms. of Sankhuwasabha and Solu Khumbu Districts in East Nepal. This park was proclaimed in 1988. This park is rich in some of the extraordinary pristine forests and alpine meadows of Nepal. The topography and geology of this park give it a rich diversity in vegetations ranging from sub-tropical sal forest to alpine pastures between 4000 to 5000 meters. There are more than 50 species of animals including red panda, musk deer, ghoral, tahr, leopard.

Apart from the above National Parks there are three Wildlife Reserves, namely Sukla Phanta Reserve (305 sq. kms.), Parsa Reserve (499 sq. kms) and Koshi-Talpu Reserve (175 sq. kms) for preserving the national resources of Nepal. These reserves provide outstanding panorama and feature of Nepal's singular beauty and charm for international visitors. The economic value of tourism is adjusted to the ecological and biological activities for making these areas to scientific, inspirational, educational and recreational welfare of the people of the world to progress and to the advancement.

Sukla Phanta Reserve is located in the south-east corner of Nepal in the riverine plain of the Mahakali river, full of open grassland, sal forest, Khair and sissoo forest and mixed deciduous vegetations. Certain measures of protection afforded in this area since 1965 but it was officially gazetted in 1976. The open grassland is the habitat of the swamp deer (carvue duvaucell) in large numbers. Other ungulates include the spotted deer, hog deer, blue bull, wild dog, wild boar, jackal, porcupine and other. A small numbers of tigers are also sighted along with wild elephants. This reserve holds in total about twenty-five different species of mammals and number of migratory and residential birds. There is the Rani Tal (lake) in the reserve and this lake attracts herons, ducks, storks, King fishers and egrets.

Parsa Reserve to the east of Royal Chitwan National Park was famous for big game hunting and for the dense forest known as Charkoshi Jhadi. It occupies parts of Chitwan, Makwanpur, Parsa and Bara district in Central Nepal. The actual landscape of the reserve is the Churia Hills running east-west. The forest is 'Sal' dominant, Chir, pine grow in the Churia Hills and along the river. This reserve being wide supports wild elephant, tiger, leopard, sloth bear, gaur, blue bull, wild dog, sambhar, chital, hog deer, barking deer, ratel, palm civet and jungle cat. Different species of birds like peacock, jungle fowl, black partridge and geese seen swarming on the ponds and great rivers of the Terai. The snakes including Cobra, Karate are also found.

Koshi-Tappu Reserve is smallest reserve in the Koshi flood plain in the eastern Terai. This reserve is situated in the Terai flood plain of Koshi river. The Savannah grassland and swamps are the habitat of wild buffalo (arna). The large number of ponds and pools created in the process of constructing the eastern part of the Koshi Barrage attract a large number of fish-eating birds in the reserve. There are two Conservation Areas namely Annapurna (2600 sq. kms) and Makalu-Barun (2330 sq. kms). Nepal has taken a remarkable step to attain the objectives of nature conservation by the establishment of the King Mahendra Trust for nature conservation. Blessed with the patronage of His Majesty the King of Nepal, the King Mahendra Trust for nature conservation is an autonomous non-profit making organisation for the purpose of conserving, preserving and managing nature and its resources in order to improve the quality of life of the human population. Annapurna Conservation Project is the largest project undertaken by King Mahendra Trust for Nature Conservation in cooperation with World Wildlife Fund (WWF). Many conservation steps have been taken under the project to save the forest and wildlife in Annapurna Area. Villages have also incorporated to protect their environment as a part of a unique conservation experiment around the world deepest valley. Annapurna Conservation Area is the most magnificent ecologically significant and heavily trekked areas of Nepal and so this project has been started with a view to promoting and managing tourism in Annapurna and for proper utilization and management of the national resources of the region. Nepal has now engage to implement its task by bringing about a greater awareness to the need of preservation of natural sources and environment.

Makalu-Barun Conservation Area have covered many potential areas of natural importance and value. So there is an effort to reserve and to reduce the damage on account of population and economic growth on natural and other resources. This area is set aside as a National Park and Conservation for the benefit and enjoyment of mankind due to its outstanding natural beauty and recreational potential in the present and as well as for the future. Physically, this

Conservation Area is located to the 435 meter low gorge of Arun and Sankhuwasabha up to the 8463 meter Makalu Himalayan peak, the fifth highest peak in the world. The area is rich in diversity. There are many lovely villages inhabited by different ethnic groups. Barun Valley is also equally celebrated for its wilderness full of virgin forests. Plant life unique to the area include oak, mapple, magnolia, fir, birch, rhododendrons, juniper and many other species. There are more than 50 species of animals including red panda, musk deer, ghoral, thar, leopard possibly snow leopard, serow, barking deer, black bear, wild boar etc. It is also the home of the rare kinds of plants and orchids, birds and butterflies, mammals and other wildlife. This area is also rich in water resources and contains 84 varieties of fishes. This Conservation Area includes zone of strictly controlled natural reserve and residents live in harmony with nature.

While taking the subject of wildlife in Nepal, one should not forget to mention one Hunting Reserve named as Dhorpatan (1325 sq. kms). This reserve is in the district of Rukum, Baglung, Myagdi in Central Nepal. This reserve is for hunting blue sheeps and other game animals. The natural vegetations of the reserve consist of pine, fir, birch, hemlook, rhododendron, oak, juniper and spruce Mammals such as leopard, ghoral, serow Himalayan thar, Himalayan Black bear, barking deer, wild boar etc are plenty in the reserve. Pheasants and partridges are common. This reserve permits controlled hunting. This reserve has endangered species such as red panda and cheer pheasants and they are protected species.

Realizing the substantial international implications happening out of Tourism from the transfer of wealth which results from the money earned to the country is spent in the development of the region and the people living in it, Nepal has embarked for the development and realistic planning of her natural resources through National Parks and Conservation Areas.

13

Tourism Development and Natural Resource Issues

Nepal is Nature lover's paradise. Many international visitors travel to Nepal to be in the calm and tranquill atmosphere of nature. It is a country of mountains and a very pleasant climate. Every type of climate is found here from the plains of the Terai in the south bordering India to the summits of the Himalayas in the north. The country has from tropical to alpine climate due to extreme variations in altitudes. Naturally, it has tropical, sub-tropical to alpine type of vegetations and a rich and varied species of fauna. It is credited with the grandeur of the great heritage of forests, mountains and rivers. The scenic beauty of Nepal is associated with all things that gives visual pleasure. Natural panorama is an essential element for tourism. Due to its physiographical frame, Nepal unfurls natural and scenic attractions of exuberant forms and beauty. Chipping in plenty of extraordinary phenomenon posing dashing and diversified views not to be seen in any other parts of the globe. It is these singular feature which cover some of the earth's most impressive tourist attractions. Nepal holds a unique place in the tourist maps of the world with many more breath-taking wonders of natural grandeurs of the green hills and valleys with the snow-capped Himalayas reposing out of the world marvels. Enchanting scenes of the natural wonders silhouetted by lush green environs everywhere with sprouting vegetations and variety of flowers in full blooms.

It is also botanically and zoologically, one of Asia's richest areas. It is a nature's play-ground all the year round providing grandeur of landscape with forests basking under the blue sky, row of green, mountain ranges circling them and glacier carrying white streams which provide a mystical charm of its own.

Nepal, no doubt, is the destination—the ultimate in adventure tourism. The prospects for adventure tourism are greatest in the Nepal where altitude, topography and climate supply ideal pre-requisite for such activities. The foremost and eminent resource of adventure tourism in Nepal is snowy Himalayas. The Himalayas constitute one of the noble features of the Nepali landscape. The Himalayan chain is an inspiring wonder of snow-covered summits, lofty cliffs, outrageous glaciers, zigzag rivers, deep and narrow gorges. The middle hills and the valleys also provide closest scenario of the snowy mountains, narrow-crested hills in knots, trackless crests and placated ravines, narrow valleys with ethnic settlements and their gay faces and costumes. Fast flowing rivers are seen in a tangle of coils, pushing and foaming create breath-taking fantasy. These are also many deepest gorge cut by tectonic snow-fed rivers giving enchantment of the picturesque valley into a magnetic attraction for nature lovers. Nepal has big tourism potentials. About the vast and alluring attractions of Nepal, it is better to quote here the expressions put forward by Han Suyin in her book—"The Mountain is Young" as written below:

> "Green and yellow fields, like a pattern upon a bee's wing, little ochre farm houses, many roofed pagodas, pink brick houses in clusters, large white colonnaded mansoons with formal gardens. It was so incongruous, to go to the Himalayas in an airplane and find a golden valley like Switzerland or northern Italy and a city in its middle that was a Hollywood dream of Cathay."

Only the cliches of tourism could describe it: smiling Kathmandu, Sunlit Nepal, and of course Shangri-la, Shangri-la." Nepal has so big tourist attractions but the country and the people aware of these potentials and concern of their upkeepment and protection. Knotty points of subjects of concern of tourism in Nepal are posing landscape and regional planning, social issues, city tourism, urbanisation induced traffic, air traffic and sound pollution and proper tourism management in enterprises etc. It is a proven fact that tourism and natural resources management as it appears that they are opposite on one hand and on the other tourism is always concerning to increase the influx of tourist with little concern for the physical impact of tourist, the extent of the seasonal pattern of density, increased space requirement produced by raising the quality, and construction of high rise buildings, highways, hotels and lodges and many ills of urbanisation without any environment assessment. Nepal should try to blend tourism with nature with the modern development of the country. Tourism development should not set aside the natural phenomenon simply because Nepal's enigma and natural beauty draw out visitors from all over the world who come to experience for themselves its uniqueness as a holiday destination. Needless to say, urban areas of Kathmandu Valley and Pokhara Valley represent major tourist centres but all to often it is implicit that urban developments exclude natural beauty from consideration. Some measures are used in the Kathmandu Valley and Pokhara Valley to protect scenic beauty by means of Land Zoning. Land Zoning has the potential of being a most effective tool in preventing tourism development for having undesirable effects on natural beauty. Local people are also now concerned about the preservation of natural beauty. Tourism development causes the use of land in an area of scenic beauty by developing of recreational facilities. The local people have a right to expect the land which will be developed in good taste. While developing tourist areas, realization must be on Land Zoning and upkeeping of scenic grandeur intact which contribute to giving the people of the areas the overall satisfaction of knowing that the natural resources and beauty of the landscape will not be misused.

Nepal offers an appealing package to North American and Westerr European tourists; an enticing climate, fascinating and unique indigenous culture, a wealth of historic and religious features and a diverse landscapes that include Himalayan mountains, tropical low-lands with dense jungles and of course lovely valleys and dales. But many of these resources are potentially exposed to danger management. It is foremost essential to identify and protect attractions and subsequently proceed with controlled and planned development. Much attention has now to be given for the environment conservation and restoration of Nepal's unique combination of natural, social and cultural resources. Earlier neglect of these important assets of tourism has lead to severe environmental deterioration. The more local manifestations of native culture especially unique architectures as expressed in temples, monasteries, lodges and even in private houses shops and old city squares are frequently allowed to decay and they are unmannerly or uniquely demolished for the sake of urbanisation. It is the need of the hour to make use of tourism planning and development as a tool for the upliftment of a wide variety of social, cultural, and ecological resources, resulting in greater balance and harmony at the regional and national level. Tourism planning should therefore, reflect the local human, social, cultural and economic environment while focussing a sound natural atmosphere with socio-economic balance.

It is almost a disgrace for us not to be aware of environment conservation and heritage even as early as 1955, Mr. Tom Weir has realistically focussed all about disruptions and intrusions in the natural environment in his book—"East of Kathmandu" in the following ways:

> "What astonished us was the intense cultivation of these Nepal hillsides. Whole range of foot hills has been scalped of every vestige of vegetation and terraced from top to bottom with green rice and golden buck wheat, and everywhere on these monotonous staircases where the grim signs of soil erosion in avalanched terraces and huge gullies riven out of wasted hillsides. Houses are dotted everywhere and the paths were literally craniling with people. The foothills of Nepal are not the place for an isolationist."

As a living example of loss of natural vegetation and romantic landscape as put forward above has been going ceaselessly up to the present and the background of rare beauty crystal streams flowing amid the forest of luxuriant foilages and greens, shady trees and tall bamboo, all have been cut away to make cultivation and habitation. Soil erosion signs are common everywhere and are giving natural hazards of land slides, change of climate, water shortage, deforestation and growth in population for settlement. Environment assessment has never been given proper consideration up to the present which has caused loss of a whole spectrum of available human and natural resources. This sort of disorderly irrational and light-fingered utilization of the natural resources are going everywhere all over the country in the name of a false and destructive concept of economic development. The exploitation of the physical environment has clearly had serious impact in all most all hilly areas of Nepal. Many design facilities are disturbing the natural landscape and no measures have been taken to minimize visual disturbances which are so important for tourism. Various unique scenic landscapes in a tourist areas are not considered in their essence as all of the elements not working in harmony to bring about the maximum unity in these areas. No thinking given for developing meaningful Tourist area in terms of materials, forms, colours and purpose, which are causing pollution on recreation sides due to akward constructions. However, there is now growing awareness of these problems and preservation and even enhancement of the environment has considered to be an important component of the development plans. Tourism continues to increase in volume and diversity and to satisfy them (International visitors) necessary measures to conserve the natural environment are to be taken into account and well-managed.

It is necessary to have easy access to any new tourist areas or existing areas of tourist attraction. So the areas throughout the country that are particularly beautiful would be served by highways. The blending of tourism with natural beauty often is represented by the mis-using of highway construction with the aesthetic qualities of the landscape and such improper use of areas defined as beautiful must be saved. Therefore, highway construction must be used as an ameliorative device to improve the landscape and provide a satisfying visual experience. In the areas where the scene is beautiful, the highway construction has to intervene with the least possible damage to exploit and reveal the visual qualities of the landscape while meeting traffic requirements.

The infrastructures are needed to meet the influx of tourists in the places of tourist interests. Hotels, restaurants, shopping arcades and other recreational facilities are needed to meet visitor's requirements. So the design facilities must be utilized to minimize visual disturbances. Design facilities of infrastructures always must suit in relation to the situation and the movement of the people. Prime consideration should be given by providing harmony with regional characteristics without harming natural beauty and utilizing natural appearing construction materials. It is better to concentrate commercial and residential development in limited areas in resort development. The characteristics needed for the mountain resorts development and the proper locations for them are plenty in the various mountain regions of Nepal. There is potentiality for the growth of mountain resorts and it is hoped that some developers will now surely realize this vacuum and come across with sound judgement and planning without disturbing natural beauty. Design facilities and access should be considered for acceptable capacities. Always bear in mind that carrying capacity is a most significant consideration to any tourist destination. A private developer may always wish to build tourist resorts or a lodge or hotel. This kind of construction is compatible with good land-use practices not on copying the complex of other country just for short term gains. The local characteristics must be maintained and local people have a right to expect the land will be developed in good shape and taste. International visitors need nature as a scenic background for holidays. Therefore, Nepal has to develop more tourist areas with recreational facilities with outstanding natural beauty. Sometimes, it is necessary to prohibit public use of some areas of untouched nature in order to blend tourism with natural beauty. In addition, pollution problems are causing harm and like every human activity, tourism is a serious pollutant. So tourism development has to change methods to make a less polluting activity. All the measures should be taken to preserve and restore nature which will lead to a rise in price of recreation and tourism. It depends on the strength of blending tourism with natural beauty to maintain and preserve tourist attractions. Tourism should not give chance to spoil an area and it should be more acceptable or somehow to allocate in a way which creates less backlash.

14

Eco-Tourism for a Sustainable Future

Nepal holds within a comparatively small area of land a uniqueness of tourist attractions which is probably single and outstanding in the world. So, variety is the true delight of Himalayan travel. To the south of the country is the lowland Terai, a flat tropical belt and is played up by the deep and silent rivers. This lowland, the foot of the mountains are covered by open flat country side with tropical climate and tropical vegetation. This flat area shelters a wide variety of wildlife including some of the Asian rhinocerous, elephants, wild buffaloes, tigers and deers. From the Terai, the land rises steeply to the Mahabharat Lekh mountain range with peaks of up to 3,050 meters. This is followed by the wide bank of the Central Hills mostly steep rugged and undulating mountainous area, cut through by deep valleys. This range represents as a natural wall protecting the lower middle Hills and passing north envelops range the actual mainland bordered by the Great Himalayan Range further north. On the lower slopes of the Himalayas are situated picturesque towns, peaceful villages, and cities, serene surroundings that create a charming atmosphere. These physical frame of the country features earth most spectacular attractions and a rich varied wealth of recreational resources. Nepal, a valuable treasure house of visual delight provides a wide range of exciting and exotic sightseeing.

Nepal has varied natural attraction such as interesting configuration, unusual formation, panorama, colour of lands, rocks, gorges etc. at their best settings. The mountains and its sides of Nepal constitute the alpinism which are the biggest attractions for tourists visiting Nepal. Trekking is probably the visitor's pastime owing to the country's vast and generally safe landscapes that rise from the valleys to the majestic peaks of the Himalayan ranges. The nature lover can arrange Safari tours to the Terai on the elephant's back to observe stamped rhinos and stalking tigers. Different types of flora and fauna are preserved in Nepal's National Parks and Wildlife Reserves and Conservation areas scattered all over the country. The arrangement for Safari tours are organised for international visitors who are eager to view wild grandeurs in close angle with modern comforts. Side by side with marvellous natural attractions, Nepal is regarded for experiencing some of the greatest sites of South Asian Cultural heritage. The Country is a veritable museum of artistic treasures, magnificent shrines, temples and lavishly decorated edifices, images and carvings of exquisite design all competing with scenic mountain grandeur unequalled anywhere. International visitors are amazed by viewing the exoticism of Nepali arts and architectural wonders. Again, Nepal is multi-racial and multi-lingual country. Life style of the Nepali people act as the major attraction to visitors due to their simple and hospitable character and represent an important facet of cultural tourism. Nepal is world renowned sacred place for both Hindu and Buddhist people of the world as being the birth-places of Sita, the Consort of Lord Rama, the hero of the Hindu epic Ramayana and the birth-place of Sakyamuni Gautam Buddha who gave the world an enduring philosophy of peace, tolerance and compassion. So the country's natural, social and cultural environment is unique and ultimate tourist resources. This environment is a key asset for the tourism industry.

Eco, generally composition connected with habitat and environment in relation to living organism as in ecology. The word "ecosystem" is therefore used to describe the interaction system comprising living things together with their non-living habitats. That is why tourism without human contact becomes a destructive force and it must contact wildlife, sunshine, wilderness and nature adventure while making relationship whatever with the local people and never missing this aspects very much. In this respect, ecotourism signifies the meaning of proper management of habitat and environment in relation to all facets of society which can be a leading force in preserving the lifestyle of the people, landscape, heritage and cultures for the future. International visitors are attracted into less-visited places to see natural wonders, to experience a simple life-style and to learn about ecosystems and conservation. Uncontrolled growth in nature travel trends around the world specially due to industrialization and urbanisation of all developed nations give rise to a word as it is called ecotourism, socially responsible tourism, environmentally sensitive tourism, ethnical tourism and so on. The environment that sustains life on earth is in trouble and human actions are responsible for all these evils and the problems are many. It is high time now to endorse and implement environmentally responsible tourism. Congenial planning for different types of outdoor recreation and natural resources are essential. The important nature of the concern now for tourism in our country is the blending of tourism and ecology, i.e. ecotourism provides a setting-up of the essence of the issue: resource and social "carrying capacity", carefully planning and effective management, heritage conservation and fragility of the environment. Visits for natural environment of international tourists in our country is vital to the political, economic and social relationship between underdeveloped and developed countries so quality outdoor recreation must be developed in maximum tourist satisfaction depending on the provision of high quality natural and human environments. Favourable atmospheres underlying in the host region and outdoor recreation experience can automatically cause in new and repeat visits in our country. But of increased international visitor arrivals and the diversity of outdoor recreation behaviour patterns, outdoor recreation areas have a physical and psychological carrying capacity which so far not defined by management objectives in our country. This capacity can not be exceeded without reducing levels of user satisfaction and environmental quality. Recreation environment must be protected by appropriate and sound planning and managed to prevent diverse results using compatibility planning technique in our country in order to reduce visitor dissatisfaction and provides ample opportunity for quality recreation experiences to take place. It is for sure that if timely planning not taken, popular destinations of our country are suddenly to receive a vast decrease in tourist arrivals due to poor development and planning, over-crowding and pollution and to inadequate resources without proper planning. Proper planning with new awareness only provides alternatives to path of ultimate waste in the future in our country.

Here it is not inappropriate to mention that the diversity of vegetations and animals and their habitats in Nepal contribute the sense of uniqueness of adventure. Preservation of these resources not only helps to keep nature in balance but also provides the incentives to travel and to help visitors repeat their visits. So tourism should follow conservation side by side with the growth of tourism and not vice versa in our country. As much of natural environment must be kept in good condition for future generation of mankind and for the long term sustenance of quality tourism in our country. At the same time, our country needs to act to conserve man-made cultural heritage resources as well. The rich arts and architectural treasures of cultural past must be restored and preserved for the view of future generation of visitors to these sites. There is need to ensure that they must taste the richness of the cultures that created these monuments and have a total travel experiences by international visitors. There is utmost urgency in our country to promote awareness on the need to conserve the environment. The environment signifies here all aspects of the surroundings of human beings, both cultural, natural and man-made without affecting human being as individuals or in social groupings and all living things and non-living habitats. Conservation signifies the management of human use of the environment to provide the greatest benefit to present generations while maintaining the potential to meet the demands and aspirations of the future mankind of the world. As for development means the modification of the environment in whatever degree and the application of human, financial, living and non-living resources to satisfy human needs and improve the quality of human life, what is necessary to-day in our country is a revival of a consciousness of roots with the past within the travel and tourism industry. A renewal commitment acts sure to contribute individually and collectively ensuring heritage resources of mankind for conservation which serves as resources for tourism operations for many more generations to come. Awareness among the local inhabitants is necessary to solve environmental problems. The local residents must be involved in the implementation of tourist development. His Majesty's Government of Nepal must advocate environmentally responsible tourism by interpreting the ecology of regions and their attendant issues for international visitors, tourist industry parties and associates. His Majesty's Government of Nepal, Ministry of Tourism should take initiatives to formulate specific guidelines and standards for responsible ecotourism. It should make policy for participation of local community and all non-government organisations related with tourism's involvement in ecotourism and the wise use and management of natural areas and resources and inculcating respects for living cultures. It should promote the allocation of budgetary provisions needed for conservation and heritage preservation. Tourism planning formulated in union with the local people proves to be an efficient, realistic and necessary means to enhance environmental and cultural values and facilities for the use and appreciation of the local communities and the international visitors. Such planning will lead closer in the enhancement of ecotourism and its development.

Index